5

C

The Young Child at Home

C.E. Davie, S.J. Hutt, E. Vincent
and M. Mason

NFER-NELSON

Published by The NFER-NELSON Publishing Company Ltd.,
Darville House, 2 Oxford Road East,
Windsor, Berks SL4 1DF

First published 1984
© *C.E. Davie, S.J. Hutt, E. Vincent, and M. Mason*
ISBN 0-7005-0641-1
Code 8165 02 1

Printed in Great Britain

Distributed in the USA by Humanities Press Inc.,
Atlantic Highlands, New Jersey 07716 USA.

In memory of Corinne Hutt

Contents

Note: Further details of the research method are available on request from: Ms Charmian Davie, Department of Psychology, University of Keele, Keele, Staffordshire ST5 5BG.

Acknowledgements

This book is dedicated with great affection to the memory of Corinne Hutt, who, with John, conceived the idea from which the research project developed. Her kindness, generosity and brilliance were an inspiration to everyone who worked on this project.

We are extremely grateful to Margaret Short for her part as secretary to the project. Her contribution far exceeded the bounds of normal secretarial duties. Our thanks also to Dorothy Masters, Doreen Waters and Margaret Woodward who assisted with the final manuscript preparation amidst their normal departmental commitments.

We would like to thank the Department of Education and Science for financing the project and the very helpful discussion and guidance provided by the members of the DES Liaison Committee (Keele); Dr J S Hamilton, the Area Medical Officer of Health, Stafford Health Authority, for his help in initiating our sample selection procedures; the Stoke-on-Trent City Treasurer's Department for their computer programming assistance; the Health Visitors of Stoke-on-Trent and Newcastle-under-Lyme and the Preschool Growth Survey team, London School of Hygiene and Tropical Medicine, for their help in contacting the parents of potential subjects; head teachers of several Nursery and Infant schools and Play Group supervisors in the area who put us in touch with parents willing to volunteer their children for pilot stages in the study; and a great many colleagues at Keele who gave advice and assistance throughout the study, in particular Dr Paul Collis of the Keele Computer Centre who gave an enormous amount of his time and has written Appendix III of this volume.

This project could not have taken place without the help of the subjects and their families, to whom we are deeply indebted.

Chapter 1
Introduction

This book is a description of the day-to-day home life and experience of a sample of preschool children. The material was collected by watching the children in their own homes and examining their activities, conversations, social interactions and the toys and equipment they had available to them.

Why study young children's experiences in the home?

In the 1960s, interest in the intellectual development of young children exploded. This interest was particularly stimulated by two books, Joseph McVicker Hunt's 'Intelligence and Experience' (1961) and Benjamin Bloom's 'Stability and Change in Human Characteristics' (1964). Both authors argued that the preschool years were a crucial period in the child's intellectual development; lack of the right environmental stimulation at this time could lead to irreversible damage to the young child's intellect. At the same time, Basil Bernstein (1961) propounded the original version of his linguistic theory whereby, he suggested, there were clear cut social class differences in language. Working class people were only capable of using a 'restricted' code, whereas middle class people had access to both a 'restricted' and an 'elaborated' code. Briefly, the 'restricted' code was characterised by short, grammatically simple sentences and the frequent use of short commands, questions and categoric statements, in contrast to the more precise and complex grammar, wide and varied vocabulary and rational expansion and explanation of the 'elaborated' code. Home experience of solely the 'restricted' code offered two disadvantages – the first, confusion at school, where language was in the 'elaborated' code, the second, that the 'restricted' code was intellectually cramping. Bernstein's theory provided a plausible vehicle for the transmission of intellectual deficiency.

In 1964, President Johnson launched the Head Start programme. Massive financial aid was poured into a wide range of compensatory preschool programmes. The idea was to provide lower class, economically deprived young American children with educational stimulation which would prevent the perceived ill effects of spending their early years in intellectually impoverished environments (i.e. their homes). In this country, the Plowden Committee (1967) considered that nursery education could compensate for social deprivation. The committee also saw nursery education as having many advantages and recommended that it should be generally available to all children between three and five years. Plowden's recommendations were taken up in the Government White Paper, 'Education: A framework for Expansion' (DES, 1972) in which it was proposed that there be a great expansion of nursery education.

A variety of preschool compensatory programmes and teaching techniques had meanwhile been developed, such as the Peabody Language Development Kits, (Dunn, Horton and Smith, (1968)), the language programmes of Bereiter and Engelmann (1966) and in this country Blank and Solomon's (1969) very specific use of brief one to one tutorials for 'poorly functioning' children. A report by Cicirelli and a number of co-authors was published in 1969 and came to the depressing conclusion after examing a range of Head Start programmes that any gains made by the children during these programmes had evaporated after a year at school. Subsequent evaluation of more rigorously selected programmes (Consortium on Developmental Continuity, 1977; Consortium for Longitudinal Studies, 1978), however, have come to different conclusions and these will be discussed in the final chapter of this book.

Barabara Tizard, writing in 1974, spoke of 'the surprisingly little direct evidence ... that the talk in working class families is deficient both in quality and quantity.' We felt this to be very true. Influential studies had been made by Hess and his colleagues (notably, Hess and Shipman, 1965) on maternal/child interactions in the laboratory. They reported marked differences between upper and lower class mothers in the style of interaction with their children. Lower class mothers were more likely to allow their children to make errors which the mothers then punished. In contrast, upper class mothers anticipated their children's difficulties, drew the child's attention to them and suggested alternative strategies. Similarly, lower class mothers offered 'yes'/'no' answers to problems, whereas upper class mothers sometimes gave extensive explanations. Other laboratory-based, experimentally manipulated studies were reported by Bernstein's colleagues, Bernstein (1972), and documented marked differences in speech between middle and working class subjects.

Bernstein's original theory has been severely criticised by, for example, Rosen (1973), who argued that it was based on an inadequate concept of social class, leading to a very stereotyped view of working class life and attributed 'rare and remarkable' virtues to middle class speakers. Bernstein has subsequently substantially revised his theoretical position (Bernstein, 1975) and this is discussed in Chapter 8 of this book. Labov (1969) strongly opposed both the theoretical position and the validity of generalising from experimental evidence to speech occurring in more natural circumstances. He argued that both the language and linguistic style of working class people were strongly dependent upon their context. He collected and analysed speech from working class urban blacks that demonstrated that if the interviewer is seen as a peer, the circumstances and the subject of the conversation fall within the subject's normal realms of experience, then the subject's speech is logically precise and fluent.

The danger is that a laboratory or quasi-experimental setting may be producing or enhancing social class effects. Van der Eyken (1977) makes this point when commenting on some speech samples presented by Tough (1973) to illustrate qualitative differences in the discourse of mothers and children from 'advantaged' and 'disadvantaged' homes in order to support her theoretical position, which is closely allied to Bernstein's. The dialogues were recorded in a nursery school headmistress's waiting room. The 'disadvantaged' mother's speech consists largely of prohibitions, aimed at preventing the child disarranging or damaging the office and, while illustrating many of the characteristics of the 'restricted' code, betrays an overwhelming anxiety about the social context of the situation.

Large scale surveys have also provided information on the young child's home life. A major work of this type is the National Child

Development Study. Information was collected on some 17,000 children in infancy, then again at seven years of age, and the study is still continuing (Pringle et al., 1966; Davie et al., 1972). For this survey parents were interviewed and medical assessments and assessments by teachers were made. Another major study is that of the Newsons, conducted on approximately 700 families in Nottingham. This again is an ongoing, longitudinal study. In the preschool years, they interviewed the children's parents when the children were one and four years old respectively (Newson & Newson, 1963; 1968). Both these studies have made important contributions to our knowledge of epedemiological issues, of factors affecting school attainment and of parental perceptions of their child rearing practices. Interview studies have the advantage of being able to cover large sample numbers; once an interview or assessment tool has been designed, it is relatively easy and quick to use. In addition, large samples of children can be included as subjects, with consequently greater confidence in the generality of the findings. A major drawback to this method, however, is that an interview depends on the reliability of the respondent. When parents are reporting on their attitudes and practices in relation to their children, both the pressure of what is socially desirable and also misrecollections are likely to detract from the accuracy of the reporting. As an example, in the Newsons' initial study, 70 per cent of the sample was interviewed by Health Visitors and 30 per cent by University interviewers. With a number of questions, the results differed depending on the identity of the interviewer. For instance, parents were significantly more likely to admit to the University interviewers that they had given the child a dummy than they were to the Health Visitors. There is no absolute means of determining what effects interviewers are having on respondents' replies. Another drawback to the interview approach is that questions must be confined to those which the respondent can answer. Detailed examination of aspects of the child's social interactions or the minutiae of a child's activities are not open to investigation by interview.

A third approach is possible; watching the child and recording his behaviour in his own home. If the situation is not manipulated, this can permit the recording of both the child's naturally occurring behaviour and his family's behaviour in their natural environment. The recordings are not second hand, (i.e. through the eyes of the parent) and avoid the potential biasing effects of interviewee perceptions of both the child's and the parents' own behaviour. Direct observation also allows the examination of much subtler issues than can be explored by interview techniques. The disadvantage of this approach is that it is enormously time consuming, in terms of construction, implementation and analysis and that it demands a great deal from the subjects and their families. This inevitably leads to smaller samples than is feasible in an interview study. Moreover, while doing away with potential respondent bias, there is still the fact that the presence of an observer may alter the behaviour of the child and his family. There is again no way of definitively assessing this affect. Attempts to assess the habituation of the children to the observer are presented in the next chapter.

Following the 1972 White Paper, it seemed likely that in the next few years the majority of preschool children would be attending some form of nursery provision. If preschool education was to complement and enhance the young child's home experience, it seemed essential to have a more thorough knowledge of that experience. Two research projects funded by the Department of Education were initiated at the University of Keele in 1974, 'Young Childrens's Experiences at Home' and 'Play, Exploration and Learning'. The latter was a project designed to investigate practical and theoretical issues in the preschool. Data from this project are discussed and compared with data from the home in Chapter X of this book.

At the inception of the 'Young Children's Experiences at Home' project, there was little modern direct information on young children's behaviour at home. Clarke-Stewart (1973) had observed working class children between the ages of 9 and 18 months and assessed the quality of maternal child interaction and its relationship to cognitive, social and language measures of competence. This type of approach has been pursued by Carew and her colleagues with longitudinal studies of children up to the age of three years (Carew *et al.*, 1976; Carew, 1980). Clarke-Stewart (1980) points out the difficulty of assessing an experience as intellectually valuable to the young child. If, as in Carew's studies, intellectual value is assessed on the basis of the similarity of this experience to items in standardized intelligence tests, the assessment of the children in terms of the tests becomes circular. Dunn and Kendrick in a longitudinal study have examined the detailed changes in child and maternal behaviour at the birth of a new sibling (Dunn and Kendrick, 1980; 1981) and the relationship between the mother's behaviour to the first-born child shortly after the advent of the new sibling and later sibling interaction. Barbara Tizard and her colleagues have compared the verbal behaviour of nursery school children at home and at school (Tizard, B, *et al.*, 1980; 1982; 1983) and we will be drawing on their material for comparison with our own, later in this book.

This study was wide-ranging in its objectives. It attempts to describe the types of activities in which preschool children engage, who takes part in these activities with them, and the toys and equipment they use. Activities we felt to be of particular current interest, for example, television viewing, or specifically related to modern nursery education philosophy, for instance, fantasy play and language, are discussed in detail in separate chapters. We also observed how parents conducted the physical necessities of their young children's lives such as bathing them, feeding them and how the different types of housing the children were living in affected their lives. To increase the generality and validity of our findings, we observed a large sample of families, 165, which compares with 23 children in the Carew study and 40 families in both the Dunn and Tizard studies. We also attempted to sample the child's whole waking day, not restricting our observations to mornings or afternoons, but including early mornings, late evenings and weekends. The children were totally unrestricted while observations were made, free to move inside and outside their homes as they would have done if an observer had not been present. While the sample is large, for an observational study, it was essential to restrict it to statistically viable subgroups. Only children with United Kingdom or Eire origins were selected and children know to be suffering from a serious health defect, which would impede their normal daily living, were excluded. Furthermore, all the children had to come from households where a mother and father figure were both present.

We selected four independent variables which we considered might be potent in affecting the 'normal' preschool child's life at home. These were social class, sex, age and family position. We assessed social class in terms of the father's occupation classified according to the Registrar General's Classification of Occupations (1970). While any classification of social class is fraught with problems, the Registrar General's Classification has two advantages. The first is that it is widely used in British studies and therefore provides comparability. The sample was selected in terms of two social classes: middle class, which included the Registrar General's social classes I, II and III Non-manual, and working class, which included social classes III Manual, IV and V. The second advantage is that the Area Medical Health Records from which we proposed to draw the sample were computerised with paternal occupations coded in an approximation to this classification. The age range was selected to span the usual period of preschool provision, 3–4½ years, and subdivided into three age groups, so that maturational effects could be compared. Sutton-Smith and Rosenberg (1970) point out the enormously complex combinations of family positions essential to achieve a strict comparison of this variable. To reduce this variability we restricted the sample to only three family positions: Eldest, Only and Youngest.

As the object of the study was to investigate children's activities in the home, all children who were attending a Day Nursery or Nursery School, full or part-time, were excluded. We decided to exclude children who were going to Play Group for more than two sessions a week for two reasons: firstly, very frequent Play Group attendance might arguably be providing the child with an experience essentially similar to that of part-time Nursery School attendance, and secondly, when more than two mornings or afternoons are taken out of a child's week, it severely curtails the amount of 'every day' time he spends at home. However, we decided to include children who were looked after in the home by people other than their mothers. In our pilot study we frequently found that a number of other people besides the mother were involved in the care of the 'home' child. Parents dovetailed their work hours so that the father was at home while the mother worked, went shopping or got on with her housework. Neighbours were used for varying periods. Often payment for this assistance was in kind. We encountered a variety of combinations of those types of arrangements and decided it was invalid to make a particular cut-off point. Therefore, the sample includes a few children who were attending what would legally be defined as childminders (some of whom were unregistered) for varying periods in their normal week. Details of our sample selection procedure are described in the next chapter.

Chapter 2
Method

A Sampling procedure

Children were selected from the Area Health records for the City of Stoke-on-Trent and immediately adjacent areas. Permission was received from the DHSS and the Area Medical Officer of Health for indirect access to these records (which are computerised) for the purposes of sample selection. As we required a sample balanced according to our independent variables, the City Treasurer's programming division very kindly wrote two programs on our behalf. As circumstances can change rapidly in the life of a pre-school child in terms of our sample criteria, for example an Only child becoming an Eldest or a child unexpectedly going off to Nursery School or Class, and because we did not want to overload our intermediaries, the Health Visitors, seven runs of these two programs were made over a three year period. The first program gave the total number of children available in any one of the subgroups defined by the independent variables and children previously selected were excluded from subsequent runs. The second program took the total number of children available for each subgroup and divided this number by the total number of children required at that date for that subgroup, thus giving us a sampling frequency matched to the available number of children. This could result, for example, in the selection of every fifth child for subgroup A and every sixteenth for subgroup B. We were therefore pursuing a stratified random sampling procedure.

Health Visitors visited the prospective sample children and asked parents if they would allow their children's names to go forward to the project team. These visits involved the Stoke-on-Trent Health

Visitors in considerable extra work. The London School of Hygiene and Tropical Medicine were undertaking a Preschool Growth Study in several areas, including Stoke-on-Trent and their study covered an entire birth cohort of Stoke-on-Trent children, which included the children of the age appropriate to our sample. It was therefore agreed with the Local Health Authority that the LSHTM team replace the Health Visitors as our intermediaries. Eighty-seven of the children in our final sample were contacted by Health Visitors, 78 by the LSHTM team.

A total of 1,183 families of subjects were contacted by these intermediaries. The majority of the children who were *not* used in the study were rejected because they were attending Nursery or Infant School, were going to Play Group for more than two sessions a week, were found to come from single parent families, the computer birth order classification was out of date (i.e. the child was no longer an Only or a Youngest), or, in a few cases, the child was found to be handicapped. Problems which added to the number of children rejected from the study were that the Health Records, although based on the Registrar General's Classification, made no distinction between manual and non-manual workers in Social Class III, and that paternal occupations were coded by clerks from brief job descriptions filled in by medical personnel and only according to the

Table 2.1 Comparison of paternal occupation social class coding by Health Authority and project team

Agreements

Social Class	I	II	III	IV	V	Total
Health Authority	1	2	21	7	0	31

Project Team		NM	M		
		5	16		

Disagreements

Social Class	I	II	III	IV	V	Total
Health Authority	I	5	9	26	3	43

Project Team	I	III N	III M	I	II	IV	I	II M	III	V	III M	IV
–	2	1	2	2	5	2	1	1	23	1	2	1

five main headings, without specifically checking each occupation in the Registrar General's Classification. Table 2.1 compares the coding of 74 fathers by the Local Health Authority and by the Registrar General's Classification after the parents had been interviewed by the project team.

Disagreements in social class coding make it difficult to estimate whether any particular social class group were under-represented in the final sample due to the parents being more unwilling to participate in the study. Initially, we had hoped to subdivide the group of parents into those who did not want to participate for social reasons, i.e. because they did not like the idea, and those whom circumstances prevented them from participating. It quickly became apparent that we could not separate these two groups of parents. One parent would provide a domestic reason for not participating which another parent would point out as a problem but which they were determined to overcome. People's perception of circumstances appeared to conform to their level of enthusiasm for taking part in the study. A total of 227 children's parents would not, or could not, participate in the study, i.e. 19 per cent of the total contacted. A very large number of these parents appeared to the project team to have 'genuine' reasons, such as illness in the immediate family or of a close relative which disrupted the family's normal domestic routine and made scheduled visits impossible or parents who were decorating the house or going away on holiday and only willing to participate in the study after these events by which time the child would have crossed the relevant age barrier. For the above reasons it is difficult to make any reliable estimate of whether a particular social class group was comparatively unwilling to participate in the study.

Table 2.2   Paternal occupation social class coding of parents unwilling to participate in the study

Social Class	I	II	III	IV	V	Total
	3	20	145	47	12	227

It is likely that the majority of Class III families are IIIM and that a proportion of the fathers allocated to Class IV and V should be coded in Class IIIM and IV, respectively. In addition, there may be a number of less consistent coding discrepancies.

B The preliminary and pilot studies

A body of data was built up from extensive notes on eight 3–4½-year-old children who where observed in their homes over extended periods of time. Using this data we designed both an interview schedule and a check-list. Relevant literature was also consulted in the design of interview questions and behaviour categories.

Both the interview and the check-list were then piloted on a sample of twenty-eight 3–4½-year-old children. The sample was balanced for sex and social class, the latter following the same division as described for the Main Study in Chapter I. In the light of the pilot study, the interviewers' schedule and check-list were extensively revised.

The pilot study was crucial for the design of measuring instruments, but it was also conducted to answer other questions. We wished to know, for example, what period of time would adequately sample an individual child's waking day, how this time should be split into observation sessions, how these sessions should be arranged to sample adequately different days and what was the effect of the observer's presence upon the child and his family and how could this be minimised.

Twenty of these 28 families were asked to keep what we called 'Maternal Diaries'. Fifteen mothers kept them for two weeks, five mothers for one week and all were provided with one sheet per day with a line for each half hour period. On these, mothers were asked to jot down in two or three words what their child had been doing every half hour. Calls were made every two to three days by an observer to check if things were going smoothly. Inevitably, the reliability of these diaries is questionable, but they gave a good overall description of major routine events in the child's life. It became apparent that most of the children had both a daily routine and a weekly routine. Times of getting up and going to bed, meals and some domestic events such as going with mother to take and collect an older sibling to and from school, were fixed daily occurrences. Superimposed on this daily routine pattern was the weekly routine, in which the mother might always make a short expedition to the local shops on Monday morning and a major expedition to a supermarket on a Thursday morning when the child accompanied the mother on the Monday but on Thursday played at a neighbour's house with a friend. Particular relatives or friends were visited or came to the home on specific days and other days were for a particular domestic chore which affected the child's own activities. If the father's work hours varied across days, this affected the child's daily routine. Individual children rose from and went to bed at very different times, but the sample had a mean waking day of 12.05 hours, SD 0.15 hours.

As a result of the diaries, we observed each of the 28 children for 24 hours. Twelve two-hour observations were scheduled to cover a total of two waking days for that individual child, i.e. involving 12 visits by the observer on twelve different days with two visits covering the same two-hour period on different days. Sessions were planned to cover adequately the varying weekly events in the life of the child.

A number of check-list measurements were taken to see how the child's behaviour towards the observer altered across sessions. Behaviour such as 'mini' social play with the observer, aggression towards the observer (such as spitting at or hitting her with a milk bottle carrier) and positive physical contact (such as cuddling up to her or holding her hand) did occur. However, they were very infrequent and usually precipitated by an idiosyncratic external event, therefore no evidence of a trend across sessions could be deduced. Two of the measurements occurred sufficiently frequently across all the sample to permit statistical analysis: these were talking to and watching the observer. 'Talking to' was measured by recording whether it did or did *not* occur in any one 30 second interval. 'Watching' was scored if it occupied more than 15 seconds in any one 30 second interval. We had attempted to measure 'watching' which occurred as short peeps occupying only .5–1.0 seconds, but found recording this was too unreliable.

Neither the total amount of talking nor of watching varied with either social class or sex. There is a slight tendency for some children to be 'watchers' and others 'talkers'. While both talking and watching declined in later sessions (see Figure II.1), the main difference is that the children did more observer watching in the first session of all, than any later sessions. This is not true of talking to the observer. It was feasible that some children started as 'watchers' and, as they became used to the observers, began to talk to them. However, further examination of the data does not bear this out. Relatively high frequencies of talk erupt in individual sessions and with certain individual children. It seems likely that these were precipitated by outside, idiosyncratic, events. Elder siblings occasionally showed veiled hostility to the observer, such as muttering comments like 'I suppose *she's* got to come too', or nonchalantly shutting a door in the observer's face. Sometimes this appeared to be because the older child was jealous of the attention the subject was receiving. One six-year-old brother had given the observer a clear impression that he found her presence unwelcome, but when she finally said 'Goodbye' he said, in tones of great disappointment, 'But I thought you would come and watch me now.' On many occasions an older sibling would not have been at home coincidentally with observation sessions until several had passed. In such a case the newly arrived older sibling provided a new and unpredictable stimulus to the situation.

Anecdotally, the subjects were surprisingly acquiescent and undisturbed by the observers' behaviour. Mothers of shy children often expressed doubt about whether their child would behave naturally when the observer was present. However, this type of child seemed unstressed by the situation, apparently because the observer made no attempt to talk to or interact socially with the child. On the other hand, extrovert, chatty children were in some ways more difficult to deal with. Observers adopted a policy of smiling, nodding and making monosyllabic replies which usually had the effect of gradually reducing conversation. In a street one day an observer was following a subject who played with several children. A new child joined the group, looked at the observer and was about to speak to her when another small boy turned and said to the new child 'It's no good speaking to her, all she'll do is ... (affecting a grinning grimace) ... and say 'h'mm'. As is mentioned in the chapter on childrearing practices, children were also prepared, in the presence of an observer, to behave differently from when a 'normal' adult was about.

As the study involved considerable tolerance and assistance on the part of the parents, we piloted very carefully how to explain to them what the study was about and what we wanted from them. Often this initial conversation could take half an hour and it was impossible to have a set speech prepared. We therefore concentrated on a list of points to convey to parents and particular words and concepts to be avoided. The study was described as a survey to see what children 'did' in the home, and the term 'play' was never used since it was likely to produce the reaction 'Now play for the lady'.

Figure 2.1   Habituation of child to observer

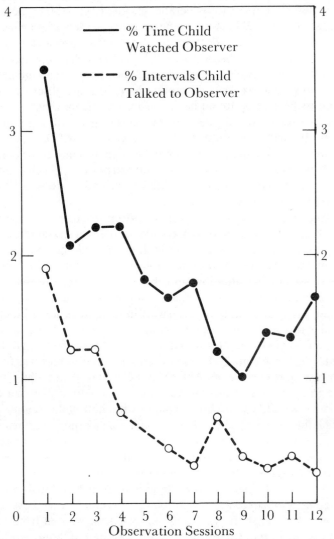

Observation Sessions

To see if some children were more inclined to talk and others to watch, a Pearson Product Moment Correlation was performed; although there is a negative correlation this does not approach significance. An analysis of variance (repeated measures) gives an overall significant difference across sessions for both talking ($F = 2.64$; $P<.005$) and watching ($F = 7.13$; $P<.001$). However, a Scheffé analysis suggested that only 'watching observer', comparing the first session with all subsequent sessions, shows a significant difference ($S = 3.55$; $P<.01$).

Similarly, the term 'behaviour' was avoided as this gave rise to parental comments such as 'Oh, he's a good boy'. We explained that many children now were attending Nursery Schools but there might be things which children were benefiting from at home which were not available at school and it was in order to examine this possibility that we were doing the study. Children with older brothers and sisters, Only children and children with younger brothers and sisters would all have different experiences and this was something else we wished to look at. Parents were fearful that somehow we had selected their child because he was abnormal in some way. We adopted the practice of always saying we were studying 'happy, healthy, normal children'. We stressed to parents that we would not interfere in anything the child was doing unless he was about to hurt himself or another child and that they were in no way to restrict the child's movements, but were to allow him to go wherever he would normally go and we would follow. If they wished to take the child with them shopping or elsewhere in a scheduled observation session then the observer would come too. We also asked parents if they would try to pretend we were not there, and we regretted that, since watching the child and writing things down required a great deal of concentration, we would be unable to talk.

Understandably, parents took a little time to adjust to this bizarre social situation. Mothers would ask the observer anxiously at the end of the first session if they were 'doing it right?' often commenting that it seemed so rude to ignore the observer. No measures were taken on parental habituation to the observer, but incidents occurred which convinced the observers that parents did often forget their presence. Intimate family affairs were often discussed freely in front of observers, parents had rows in the observer's presence and were quite prepared to undress partially and carry out such intimate personal routines as strip washing, all while observation was going on. Observers adopted the practice of ostentatiously clicking their stop watches at the end of the sessions to indicate to the parents that they were in communication again. Although we had told parents clearly that we would follow the children wherever they went, there was some embarrassment involved in following a child uninvited into (for instance) his mother's bedroom. Consequently, observers always briefly asked permission to enter any new room or area and once having been there then assumed that they could enter on future occasions.

Given our data from the pilot study on the child and on his family's habituation to the observers's presence, we decided that, firstly, an observer's presence in the home did not disrupt the child's behaviour in a way which would invalidate data collection and, secondly, that a dummy observation session was needed to give the child and his family time to adjust to the observer's presence. We decided that an adequate sample of the child's behaviour would be collected from six one-hour observation sessions. These sessions must span the individual child's waking day and his individual daily and weekly routines. In addition, the subjects should be balanced within the groups determined by the independent variable in terms of odd and even hours throughout the individual child's 12 hour waking day.

C Study Schedule for individual cases

1 Contact visit

If parents were known to be on the telephone, a time for the observer's first visit which was convenient to them was arranged. Other parents were contacted by house calls at times the intermediary had recorded as convenient. Often it was found necessary to make more than one contact visit.

2 Interview

When the parents had given their permission for their child to take part in the study, we arranged an interview either with them or with the mother alone. This might take place, if it was convenient for the parents, at the time of the contact visit. Parents were asked biographical questions about the child and the rest of the family. It was at this point that it was sometimes revealed that the child did not fulfil our sample requirements. We asked questions concerning the child's daily and weekly routines and those of his family, about proposed arrangements for the child's preschool and primary education, and about attitudes to the different forms of preschool provision. The observer would then arrange a time which suited the family for the preliminary observation session.

3 Preliminary observation

The data from this session were not used. It was used purely as a period of habituation to the observer for the child and his family. The session lasted a minimum of 30 minutes. If the child or a member of the family seemed particularly conscious of the observer, or something untoward occurred, observation was continued for a maximum of one hour. At the conclusion of the session the observer produced a timetable of the proposed six observation sessions to follow and asked the mother to check the dates and times to ensure they were feasible. At each visit the time of the next visit was again checked.

4 Observation sessions I to VI

Six one-hour observations were made. Each session was planned for a different time on a different day and we attempted to restrict the period between observations to two days. In a few cases where a child was ill or a mother forgot the appointment, the period between sessions was more than two days. Most parents enjoyed a chat with the observer after each session and it was at these times that observers learned a great deal anecdotally about the child.

5 Stanford-Binet Intelligence Test

This test was administered to the child in his own home (by the observer who had recorded his behaviour) after completion of the last observation session, either immediately after this session or on a separate visit. After the test, the observer played and talked to the child and gave him a toy to thank him for his forbearance and to persuade him that she (the observer) was normal.

D Measuring instruments used in the Main Study

1 The Check-list

Details of the behaviour definitions and time sampling procedures are found in Appendix I, as well as a copy of the check-list itself.

Items on the check-list are discussed where they appear in the relevant chapters. The way in which toys and equipment available to the child were recorded is described in Chapter IV.

2 Inter-observer reliability on check-list items

Three of the authors were responsible for collecting the data. All three were present at the inception of the project and actively engaged in the design of the check-list and formulating the behaviour category definitions. During the pilot study any categories which had low inter-observer agreement were rejected or re-formulated. Assessing inter-observer reliability in the home poses problems. The child and the family inevitably felt more inhibited by the presence of two strangers compared with one, with the result that it was difficult to get an adequate display of all behaviour categories from subjects. In an attempt to circumvent this problem we arranged for the parents of a preschool child to take video tapes with an automatic camera. In addition we had hoped to use these tapes for assessment of observer drift at various stages throughout the study. However, initial inter-observer comparisons using the tapes gave extremely low reliabilities. We examined the discrepancies and found that they were a product of the video tape. Although a wide angle lens was used, when compared with an observer's natural range of vision, this was very restricted. Inter-observer discrepancies occurred in terms of speech and interaction with the child and in a range of categories dependent on information outside the scope of the lens. We therefore abandoned video tapes as an inter-observer reliability check technique.

In 12 sessions in which each observer was paired four times with each of the other two observers and using the check-lists only, inter-observer reliability assessments were made in the form:

$$\frac{\text{Total Number of Agreed Recordings}}{\text{Total Number of Recordings}}$$

and yielded an overall mean of .78.

Inevitably there will have been fluctuations in the reliability of each observer. A 7.00 am observation may have its effect on the most conscientious observer. If an observer had a doubt as to where to record some behaviour she had observed, the problem was always noted down immediately and discussed between the three observers as soon as possible.

3 The interview and items assessed after observation was completed

Interview questions and post observation assessment items are described at appropriate places in the text. Full details of specific assessment items are given in Appendix II.

E Computer processing

The processing of the check-list data in order to shape it into a form on which conventional statistical packages could operate is described by Dr Paul Collis in Appendix III. Other data were conventionally coded for immediate manipulation by SPSS (Statistical Package for the Social Sciences) and BMDP (Biomedical Computer Programmes).

F Statistical analysis

The majority of the analyses involve frequency comparisons between the groups defined by the independent variables and a four-way Analysis of Variance was used. It was found necessary to make a logarithmic transformation to achieve homogeneity of variance and normality of distribution. Where distributions were very negatively skewed, Analysis of Variance was inappropriate and x^2 has been applied to the number of individuals involved. Inevitably this results in some loss of information. As a large number of statistical tests of significance are involved in the analysis, it was decided that the null hypothesis would be rejected at levels of significance of less than .01. Where differences approach this level, it is mentioned in the text and in particular cases details are given in the tables. The Scheffé test was used for multiple comparisons between means. Both Winer (1970) and Ferguson (1971) point out that the Scheffé procedure is more rigorous than other procedures and suggest that the investigator follow Scheffé's (1953) recommendation that a less rigorous significance level may be chosen, i.e. .10 instead of .05, and so this practice has been adopted.

G Summary of sample characteristics

The data described in this book is from a sample of 165 children. The sample is balanced in terms of four independent variables.

1	Social class	middle class
		working class
2	Sex	boys
		girls
3	Age	3–3½ years
		3½–4 years
		4–4½ years
4	Family position	Eldest
		Only
		Youngest

The children had no known serious health defect, were of UK or Eire origins, were not from single parent families, were not attending Nursery School, class or a Day Nursery or Play Group for more than 2 sessions a week.

Chapter 3
The children's homes and their families

A The area

The children in the study lived in Stoke-on-Trent and in areas extending approximately six miles beyond the city's boundaries. The city is situated in the middle of North Staffordshire. Pottery manufacture, established in the eighteenth century, is still its primary employment industry and local firms include internationally known names such as Wedgwood, Royal Doulton, Spode and Minton. The second most important industry is coal mining, while the Michelin Tyre Company Ltd have their UK headquarters in the city and are the largest single employer. Other heavy and light industries consist of iron works, foundries, chemical works, engineering plants, rubber works, paper mills and the usual construction and service industries (City of Stoke-on-Trent, 1977). Newcastle-under-Lyme now forms a continuous conurbation with the South side of Stoke-on-Trent. Much of the housing in Stoke and Newcastle is nineteenth and early twentieth century small terraced houses. The Local Authority has spent considerable effort in renovating and rebuilding this ageing housing stock. They have also built a number of large council estates and recently there has been quite a bit of private development on reclaimed or cleared land. Newcastle provides a considerable amount of suburban housing for people who work in Stoke, as do more peripheral rural areas, which serve as dormitory villages to the city. The area as a whole was generously endowed with parks in the last century, and these are beautifully maintained and the local authority has, in the past twenty years, made a great effort to deal with the waste land problem (created by clay and coal extraction) and to landscape the tips and pits and turn them into recreational areas.

Stoke has an early history of nursery education. In the 1920s infant teachers were impressed by the work of the McMillan sisters and founded a branch of the Nursery School Association in 1929. In 1931 the first Nursery School was opened (City of Stoke-on-Trent, 1960). War nurseries were opened in the Second World War because women in the area were needed for work in the munitions factories and the pottery industry which was an important source of foreign exchange. The 1944 Education Act accelerated post-war preschool provision, making it a duty for Local Education Authorities to provide Nursery School accommodation if the area needed it. The high proportion of women pottery workers made this necessary. At present there are 21 Nursery Schools, 53 Nursery Classes and six Day Nurseries within the area.

B Housing

The dwellings of the sample reflect the housing in the area. Fifty-seven per cent of both classes lived in semi-detached houses. Most of the recent council and private building in the area is of semi-detached houses. A higher proportion of the working class families lived in terraced housing while more middle class families lived in detached homes. Only 2 per cent of the families lived in flats and these were all first floor flats. This is consistent with Stoke-on-Trent's declared policy not to house families with small children in high-rise apartments.

Five per cent of the working class families (all living in old terraced houses) lacked indoor lavatories and a fixed bath or shower. These families all had flush lavatories in the backyard. In addition, one of these families had to heat their water by boiling a kettle. All households had sole use of their toilet facilities and kitchens, with the exception of one middle class family who had grandparents living with them in a partially separate flat. Overcrowding was not a real problem. Only 2 per cent of the entire sample were living in conditions of over 1½ persons per room, which is the figure usually taken as an unacceptable level of overcrowding.

Three subjects were living, with their parents, temporarily in the homes of a close relative, grandparents or an aunt. In all cases this was because the parents were in the process of moving and there had been a hitch in buying the new house or in builders' completion dates. Two of the families were middle class and one working class. In the rest of the sample the subject's parents were the householders and the vast majority of the middle class parents were owner-occupiers. While a high proportion of the working class subjects' parents were owner-occupiers, almost a third lived in council accommodation. Owner-occupation is faciliated in this area by the large stock of relatively cheap terraced housing; in 1979 small unmodernised terraced house were selling for approximately £3000, and for £6000 when fully modernised.

'Housing estate' is a widely used expression. Where a large number of modern houses of approximately the same design are all built at the same time there is little doubt that this comprises an estate. However, small modern developments and areas of prewar suburban private housing are less clearly included. In Stoke-on-Trent, council houses have been built in broad areas uninterrupted by private housing. We therefore defined a family as living on a council estate if there were council houses both in the immediate street and in the adjacent area, while a family was considered to dwell on a private estate if there were no council or terraced houses in the immediate street or adjacent area, since all the new private building is of semi-detached and detached housing. Three per cent of the middle class families lived on council estates as opposed to 30 per cent of the working class families. In contrast, 59 per cent of the middle class families were living on private estates, as were 30 per cent of the working class families.

Some outdoor play area is clearly important for preschool children. If the area is in the household's curtilage it has obvious advantages of safety and convenience. Only one family had no outside area which was 'their own'. This family lived in a flat over a shop. Council flat dwellers had either the back or the front garden. Gardens and yards were assessed for size: 'small' was defined as 0–50 square yards and included a normal sized yard behind a terraced house; 'medium' was taken as between 50–150 square yards and included the garden area usually present with a modern semi-detached house; 'large' was over 150 square yards and, in one case, included several acres. Some of the older prewar council houses have very extensive gardens, and account for the working class children with access to large gardens. Otherwise the areas correspond to the type of housing, working class children being confined to yard-sized areas more often than middle class children, but the majority of both groups having access to medium sized outside areas (see Table 3.1).

Table 3.1   Percentage of families with different sized yard or garden area

	Middle Class	Working Class
Large	7	2
Medium	29	29
Small	10	22
None	0	1

In the pilot study it was apparent that a garage with direct access was often an importart play area. If present in a modern semi-detached house it usually opens directly off the kitchen. The mother can easily keep an eye on what the child is doing by leaving the back door open and the child can use the covered area for vigorous physical activities such as tricycle riding. However, in the Main Study, only 6 per cent of the sample, despite the high proportion of semi-detached dwellings, had this facility. Predictably, a high proportion of the working class families (35 per cent of the sample) did not have a garage at all, because they are frequently not provided in council accommodation and there is no space available in terraced housing.

Another aspect of the enviroment which directly affects the young child's activities is the amount of traffic passing his home. We divided the 'busyness' which described the road or street to which the child's home had access into three assessments; Very Busy, comprising major trunk roads, main thoroughfares, heavy commercial vehicles, dense private traffic; Busy, with no heavy transport except service vehicles and local through traffic; Quiet, where the traffic came only to the immediate vicinity and/or two or three other adjacent streets. Only 6 per cent of the children were living adjacent to very busy roads, while 72 per cent were next to quiet streets.

C Affluence

Rateable values are available for public inspection and provide an approximate indication of the family's affluence. Twenty-seven per cent of the families were living in houses with a rateable value over £200. Of these, 24 per cent were middle class, 3 per cent working class.

We also monitored ownership of selected items which both affect the child's environment and indicate the parents' affluence. In the pilot study, one middle class family deliberately did not have a television set but in the Main Study all 165 families had sets. In the pilot study, one family lived in a very decrepit, damp, unmodernised house and had no table which could be called a dining table. This we selected as a criterion of lack of furniture and therefore as 'impoverishment'. We defined dining table as a table at which more than one person could sit, although frequently the table was never actually used for meals. Two of the working class families did not own a table of this type. There was a class difference in terms of telephone ownership: 82 per cent of the middle class parents had telephones as opposed to 38 per cent of the working class parents. Car ownership also showed a class difference – 'ownership' included any private access to a vehicle thus including private cars provided by a firm and commercial vehicles which could be used by the family on private outings. Only three middle class families did not own a car, while nearly a third of the working class families did not. A large proportion of the middle class had more than one vehicle.

D The father's social class and work

Information in this area was obtained during the parental interview, except where stated differently.

The father's social class was assessed according to the Registrar General's Classification of Occupations (1970). The sample mirrors the 1971 Census figures for the area. In the middle class, Class II preponderates and in the working class, Class IIIM (see Table 3.2). Three of the working class fathers were unemployed and one was in prison; these were all classified in terms of their last employment.

Table 3.2   Percentage of fathers in individual social classes

I	II	IIINM	IIIM	IV	V	%
8	27	11	42	11	2	

Parents were also asked by the observer questions concerning the husband's occupation which might influence the amount of time he was able to spend with the child. Six per cent of all fathers had jobs additional to their primary employment: 2 per cent were middle class and 4 per cent working class. These jobs varied from serving petrol on Saturday morning to being a Territorial Army reservist. Middle class fathers were more likely to be involved in staying away from home overnight than working class fathers. We divided the likelihood of being away into three categories: home fathers (who made up 86 per cent of all fathers) whose jobs never took them away; short stay fathers, whose jobs, regularly or intermittently, had involved them staying overnight from home for up to three nights a week within the last 12 months (middle class 3 per cent; working class 1 per cent); and extended stay fathers who were defined in a similar way as short stay fathers, except that the length of stay involved was four or more nights (middle class 7 per cent; working class 2 per cent). A few fathers had to attend annual in-service training courses. Predominantly the middle class fathers had to stay away from home to pursue business at the managerial or sales level, while long distance lorry driving accounted for the absences among the working class fathers.

The father's work times could also be expected to affect the amount of time he was able to spend with the child. Over half the fathers regularly or intermittently worked at the weekend; 22 per cent of these fathers were middle class and 32 per cent working class. We assessed the father's normal working hours as either ordinary office hours, which included hours approximately from 9am to 5pm, or shift work. Seventy-eight per cent of the fathers worked office hours, while 22 per cent were shift workers, (middle class 7 per cent; working class 15 per cent) (this includes one working class father who was permanently on night work).

E The mother's work; past and present

During the interview we asked mothers about their current employment (if they were working) and also what previous occupation they had had. The most highly trained previous occupation was then recorded. This was to get an idea of any specialist training the mother might have had but was not currently using, such as teacher or secretarial training. We felt this gave a better indication of educational level and was more easily asked than questions concerning school-leaving age. Thirteen per cent of the mothers had held occupations classified in Social Class I or II. Of these, 11 per cent were married to husbands with middle class occupations, 2 per cent to husbands with working class occupations. Teaching was the predominant profession of these mothers. Forty-three per cent of the mothers married to husbands in either class had been in the III Non-manual group, which included clerical workers, shop assistants and a large range of occupations in the service industries. Skilled manual work, i.e. Social Class IIIM, is available locally for women in the pottery industry and 29 per cent of the mothers had had jobs within this classification. Five per cent of the mothers were married to middle class husbands and had had Social Class IV jobs (they had almost all been telephonists). A further 11 per cent of the mothers had had jobs rated as Social Class IV and V and were married to working class husbands.

If mothers were currently working we asked them what the job entailed and where it was performed. The latter is important in that, if it is a job outside the home, some form of care has to be arranged for the child. At the time of the study, 39 per cent of all the mothers were working in some capacity. More middle class mothers (22 per cent) had jobs than working class mothers (17 per cent). Where the mother was doing a different job to the one she had had before the child had been born, the social class rating for the current occupation was in all cases lower than that of her previous occupation.

Ten per cent of the mothers worked in their own homes. This work included pottery painting, commercial sewing, product packaging, and child minding. Only 9 per cent of the mothers engaged in full time work outside the home and they were all continuing the same employment they had had before they had the child. Part-time jobs outside the home were various. Examples of these were shop work, hair dressing, play group supervision, factory work and office cleaning.

F Caretakers while mothers worked

If the mother did go outside the home to work an alternative
caretaker was necessary unless she was able to take the child with
her. We included fathers as alternative caretakers, since, frequently, the mother's work was chosen in order that it dovetailed
with the father's hours. Fathers were the most common alternative
caretakers, both as the only alternative caretaker and as additional
'overlap' caretakers in the early morning, evening and at weekends
when another individual's caretaking time left a period uncovered
while the mother was still at work. Nineteen per cent of the children
were cared for by their fathers at some time while their mothers
worked and 11 per cent by relatives. Six per cent of the children
attended childminders, who were defined as such if the caretaking
arrangement came within the bounds of the Child Minders' Act. A
few children were cared for on complicated schedules. In the two
most complex 'systems', the children, far from being disturbed,
appeared to enjoy the situation. Each alternative caretaker only
had them for a short period and was prepared to make a special
effort during that time. The child knew the routine and looked forward to his time with each individual. For example, one little boy
whose mother worked as a hairdresser spend Monday at the salon
with his mother, Tuesday and Thursday mornings at Playgroup, and
Tuesday afternoons with an aunt. Thursday afternoons were spent
with his mother's friend, Fridays with his grandmother and Saturdays with his father. Child caretakers were defined as under 12 years
of age. None of the sample was, according to the parents, left in the
care of children under 12, although the observers felt that in two
cases short overlap periods did exist when there was no older individual in the house. Teenagers were classified as 13–15 years old and
served in a few cases as 'overlap' caretakers for their younger siblings. Similarly, unpaid friends, who in most cases were neighbours,
helped out for short periods between mother leaving for her evening
shift work and father getting home.

G Babysitters

We asked mothers who went out regularly, i.e. at least once a week,
for non-working reasons, what arrangements they made for their

child. Only 18 per cent of the mothers said they did go out this often. Three per cent regularly attended an evening class or had a 'mum's night out' and the father did the babysitting. With the rest of the families, both the parents went out together and the most common babysitter was a close relative. Interestingly, the four working class families who used a relative all regularly took the children to their grandparents for Saturday evening and the whole of Saturday night, collecting them on the Sunday morning. A couple of families used teenagers regularly and two families used minders. In one of these families the childminder already cared for the child while the mother worked and in the other the minder had the child when the parents did their one, big, weekly shopping expedition.

H Relatives and the extended family

We anticipated that availability of relatives would be important in the child's life, especially for caretaking. As we have seen, they were used both for looking after the children while the mother worked and for babysitting. We *did* ask the parents if either or both of them had a relative living in the area, i.e. within the City or within five miles of its boundaries. Eighty-two per cent of the middle class families had maternal relatives in the area and 74 per cent local paternal relatives. The figures are very high for the working class families, 96 per cent and 94 per cent respectively. Four households included grandparents, three of these families being middle class. One of these arrangements was temporary, as described earlier. In five other families the households were again extended, with relatives and in-laws living in the parental home or the parents in the relatives home. We also recorded the number of relatives with whom the children had contact during the course of observation. Approximately 80 per cent of the working class children saw at least one adult relative in the course of observation, as did 50 per cent of the middle class children. Often grandparents or aunts had a particular day in the week when they came for a morning or an afternoon. This might take the form of a joint shopping expedition or venture to the park on nice days or mother might take advantage of the visit to go out shopping on her own.

I Parental ages

There is considerable evidence that children of very young parents are more likely to be 'at risk' than children with older parents. We felt that asking a question directly about the parent's age might jeopardise the future relationship of the observer and the parents and also we wished to avoid directing the parents' attention to themselves so possibly making them selfconscious. The figures here are therefore estimates made by the observers. Approximately 50 per cent of the parents did mention their ages to the observer in the course of conversation and the remaining ages have been estimated.

The working class parents were more frequently represented in the younger age groups. The small group of parents who were over forty at the time of the study were frequently couples where one or other of the partners had had a previous marriage or where the subject was the youngest child and there were grown-up or much older siblings (see Table 3.3).

Table 3.3   Percentage of parents in different age groups

	Middle Class		Working Class	
	Father	Mother	Father	Mother
Under 20 years	0	0	1	3
20–25 years	3	6	20	21
25–30 years	22	22	17	17
30–40 years	18	17	12	11
40 years and over	3	1	4	2

J Household cleanliness

During the pilot study we encountered a few households which were dirty. Our impression was that if the parents were too disorganised to clean the house then this disorganisation was also reflected in the way in which they brought up their children. In an attempt to obtain reliable comparisons between households, we devised an eleven point scale: no score indicated a completely clean house (see Appendix II for details of the scale). We also attempted to devise a scale for the 'obsessively' clean house, where parents severely inhibit a child's activities because of their care for the home and the furniture. We were unable to devise a valid and reliable scale of this type. Ninety per cent of the families had no score, in other words were completely clean. Eight per cent scored up to 4 points (middle class 2 per cent; working class 6 per cent) and only 2 per cent (working class) scored 5 or more points.

Discussion and conclusions

The children's housing and general physical environment was, overall, of a satisfactory standard. The children were not suffering the physical privations, due to overcrowding, found in Inner City areas and described by Pollak (1972) as existing among her sample of three-year-olds living in Lambeth, where frequently whole families were living in only one or two rooms and sharing bathrooms and kitchens with several other families. The conditions are very like those described by Bryant, Harris and Newton (1980) for under fives in Oxfordshire.

A few children living in unmodernised, old terrace houses were inadequately housed. For example, one child's home seemed exceptionally cold and damp to the observer and an older child had already died of pneumonia there. Out-door play space, largely lacking in the Lambeth sample, is an extremely important facility for a family with young children and here again this sample, as with the Oxfordshire sample, was provided for adequately. The small paved yard normally attached to a terraced house is very confined but does provide a safe fenced area for out-door physical activities; often the yard opens on to 'the backs' where people park their cars and which provide a relatively safe, convenient area for the neighbourhood children to play in. In modern semi-detached housing, architects could bear in mind the very important additional living space which a direct access garage can provide for a family with young children. Again, the furnishing of the homes were adequate, judging by our criterion of 'table possession', with only the one or two families living in inadequately furnished homes and struggling financially. One family, for instance, where the father was self-employed, was reduced to re-using tea bags and was unable to find the money for such basic necessities as washing-up liquid and scouring powder. The vast majority of homes were clean and well maintained, but a few families lived in conditions which were definitely below standard in this respect. In two of the middle class families this seemed to be a question of attitude; they appeared to consider that there were more important calls on their time than basic housework. In both these families, the father was holding a professional job and the mother also had professional qualifications and she was taking an active part in local organisations and affairs, energetically and competently. With the remaining families, it appeared to be an indication of disorganisation.

A relatively small proportion of families were affected by the fact that the father's job took him away from home overnight and this did not seem to impose a strain on the family in any individual case. Family life also was not disrupted by fathers working shifts at weekends, while the children were still not at school. Many mothers regarded shift work involving different hours on different days or weeks as an asset. They considered that their husbands saw more of their children than if they worked a 9–5 day, although obviously the position would change when the children went to Nursery or Infant School and were not at home during the day. Some problems were definitely encountered when fathers on shift work needed to sleep during the day. Mothers had constantly to keep the level of noise down in the living room and this very real problem was aggravated by the lack of adequate sound proofing in modern private and council housing (again a point which designers might bear in mind). The one family where the father's work hours definitely did impose a severe strain on the family, which rebounded on the child, was where the father worked nights only. This meant that during the week the father slept all day and during that time the mother had to suppress her noisy and active 3½-year-old son. When her husband went off to work at 7pm she was left on her own the entire evening, having already spent all day without adult company, and the situation was making her depressed and irritable. The financial inducement of night work was such that the family were loath for the father to change his hours.

While mothers were not asked directly if they would have liked a job of some sort, our impression was that a considerable number of mothers who were not working would ideally have liked a part-time job, both for financial and social reasons. They felt that a job would remove them for a short time from the home and give them the stimulation of adult company. This is not to say that many of the mothers were not content as housewives. The drop in social class between the working mothers' jobs before they had their children compared with their current employment reflects the difficulty women had in finding jobs where the working hours would fit in with their domestic responsibilities. Several women who were married to middle class husbands were prepared, as were their working class counterparts, to take poorly paid and relatively unskilled work such as office cleaning, despite the arduous hours of early morning and late evening work. There seemed to be two reasons for the higher proportion of mothers in middle class families who were working compared with working class mothers. Firstly, the middle class mothers were more likely to have a training which either encouraged them to continue their careers, or made it easier to find appropriate part-them to continue their careers, or made it easier to find appropriate part-time work. Secondly, we suspected that there was more financial pressure on a number of the middle class families. Many of the middle class fathers in junior management or clerical positions would not be earning much more than the skilled manual worker fathers, but were living a more expensive life style, as illustrated by the social class differences in terms of home, car and telephone ownership.

The sample selection criterion restricting subjects to children born of parents with UK and Eire origins will have biased the selection of subjects in favour of children with relatives in this country. However, bearing this in mind, the proportion of families who had been resident in the area for a considerable period of time and who had relatives living in the area is high, especially among the working class group. The middle class parents had possibly moved about the country more, in pursuit of the father's occupation. We suspect that this is a different picture from the family structure in the big cities, and the South East, but probably is representative of the Midlands and Northern towns. Anecdotally, teachers and social workers have reported that the picture is very similar in Nottingham, Leeds and Newcastle-on-Tyne. Availability of relatives was of great importance for mothers working outside the home and for babysitting. Where relatives were concerned, grandmothers predominated and the arrangements appeared to work generally to the mutual satisfaction of parents and relatives, grandparents being delighted to have the opportunity of seeing so much of their grandchildren. There also seemed to be no problem with the children over-identifying with their grandparents.

Of the childminders, both those who looked after subjects and mothers of subjects who were also minders, half were listed in the Local Authority's Child Minders' Register and half were unregistered. There seemed to be two types of unregistered minder: in the small number of cases encountered one type was the middle class housewife who was looking after a close friend's child when the mother was pursuing a professional career. These unregistered minders knew that legally they ought to be registered but showed a strong disinclination against what they saw as any bureaucratic interference into their own private affairs. The standard of care they provided was excellent. The other unregistered minders were providing an equivalent standard of care compared with the registered minders and what would probably be encountered in the child's own home.

In two cases, observers felt some concern. In the first, a registered minder, the parent of a subject, looked after a nurse's twin babies. Their mother worked shifts which varied between three different eight hour periods, yet she insisted that, regardless of the time of day when the children were with the minder, they should sleep in order that they should be of minimum trouble to the minder. The minder herself felt it was unfair to the children to expect them to conform to such an irregular routine, but considered that she had to follow their mother's wishes.

In the second case, an unregistered minder had two pre-school children of her own, the three-year-old subject and a four and a half-year-old son attending Nursery School part-time. She looked after the following children in the course of observations: a two year old, present at every visit; a four and a half-year-old boy attending Nursery School at the same time as her own son, who was with her from 7.30am till the start of Nursery School and also in the afternoons; a five-year-old girl who commenced halfway through the observations and attended before and after school. Halfway through the observations the four and a half-year-old boy who was minded developed measles. He appeared to the observers to be running a very high temperature and to be feeling very ill. He lay, crying for his mother, on the sittingroom settee, surrounded by all the children (because it was half term). The minder was a warm and loving women and she frequently cuddled and soothed him and made up promises to calm him. She told him that her husband, who had to go out, was just going to fetch his mother; that his mother would be there in a minute, at a time when it was mid-morning and she knew his mother would not pick him up till the evening. The other children all felt concerned for the boy and vigorously thrust toys at him or bounced on the settee to comfort him. The observer felt that the situation was far from ideal for a sick child.

One registered minder in a large council estate appeared to provide very valuable support for young mothers with babies. Her registration appeared to confer a professional status on her and during observations three young women with very young babies called to chat and ask advice. In many ways she appeared more interested and concerned with the subject than his own parents. His home was in the same street and after he had gone home to tea he returned to play in her garden. She saw this as a problem because during the day, while in her charge, he was not allowed to go outside her gate unaccompanied, but when he was normally under his parents' control she could impose no such restriction and justifiably felt considerable concern for his safety in the busy street.

Finally, the great majority of households were efficiently organised and maintained. The few exceptions who did score in the Family Cleanliness Scale appeared to divide into two types: two of the middle class families gave the observers the impression that their attitude to housework was one of indifference and that there were more important things in life, whereas with all the remaining families the observers felt that the lack of cleanliness resulted from deficient organisation and domestic inadequacy.

Chapter 4
Essential childrearing practices

Every child has to eat, sleep and be kept clean. Every parent is going to control and guide their child to behave in a way the parent finds socially acceptable. Children cry, laugh and have temper tantrums. They need affection and physical contact. While parents can choose the type and extent of play activities in which they wish the child to engage and how much or how little they participate with the child in these activities, some childcare requirements are essential and involve every child and his parents. This chapter deals with these aspects of childcare and includes the related affective areas of childrearing practices encountered in the study.

The data come from two sources: assessment from direct observation and parental replies to questions in the interview. The majority of items are observational; some of these were recorded in the 30 second time interval in which they occurred. Other items were assessed by the observer at the termination of all the observation sessions. Details of which type of observational assessment was used will be given when a particular item is discussed. We wished to avoid directing parents' attention to specific aspects of the child's behaviour and so possibly cause them to alter their own behaviour. Therefore direct questions to parents on childrearing practices were kept to a minimum and only asked where the information, for instance the length of the child's waking day, was essential to the planning of the observation sessions.

A Dummies and thumb sucking

Parents' replies to the question whether their child used a dummy might have been affected by their feeling that dummy use is socially undesirable. Consequently, the observer assessed, after the final observation, whether the subject had used a dummy at all. There is a modern trend in favour of dummy use. For instance, Spock (1955) advises 'If you feel that your baby needs a dummy and are worried only about what the neighbours or relations will say, tell the neighbours that this is a very modern practice (or tell them that this is your baby)'. Similarly, Leach (1975), more recently, writes '... slipping a dummy into the mouth of a crying baby who is *not* hungry is often very effective', although she does go on to suggest that dummy use should be restricted to rest periods and sleep times to prevent it getting in the way of oral exploration. However, dummies or comforters are still a source of social embarrassment to some parents and several mothers felt the need to justify their child's use of a dummy to the observer. One teacher's wife explained how she tried to restrict her three-month-old daughter's dummy use when in the home to times when there were no visitors. She described her embarrassment on meeting her GP in the street when her child was sucking a dummy. In her confusion, she drew the doctor's attention to the dummy and was laughingly assured that the doctor had used a dummy for all her own children. In the first observation session with a plumber's little girl, the grandmother was babysitting and the child asked for her dummy. Her grandmother replied that she could not have it, whereupon the subject said to her grandmother's embarrassment 'Can I have it when the lady's gone?'

The number of dummy users dropped significantly with age ($\chi^2 = 14.4$; d.f.2; P<0.001). Twenty four per cent of the three to three and a half-year-olds were using dummies, 11 per cent of the three and a half- to four-year-olds were doing so and none of the four-year-olds. Dummy use did not vary with social class.

As it is argued that giving a child a dummy can prevent thumb sucking, we examined the data to see if the children using dummies were less likely to suck their thumbs. Thumb sucking (in which we included any finger sucking) was recorded as a check-list behaviour category. We found that children who used dummies were as likely to suck their thumbs as those children who did not use dummies. They were also likely to spend as much time sucking their thumbs as the non-users. The 38 per cent of the children who sucked their thumbs did this for a mean time of 3 per cent of their waking day. While the incidence declined steadily across the three age groups, the decline was not significant.

B Carrying objects and comfort objects

Children were assessed as using a comfort object if an object was held or carried around on more than one occasion and not used in any other play activity. It was impossible to make this assessment except in 'post hoc' terms. Therefore a behaviour category 'Auto-manipulate minus look' defined as 'not looking at object while holding, manipulating, mouthing' was recorded on the check-list and the object in question was also recorded. Subsequently, all objects held in this way were listed out and those recurring on two separate observation sessions were categorised as comfort objects. Children, in our sample, spent 13 per cent of their day clutching a wide range of items, such as scraps of paper, matchboxes, teaspoons and small toys, which they were not currently using in their activities. There was a tendency for this 'general clutching' behaviour to decline with age, but this is not a significant drop.

Ten per cent of the sample were observed to use a comfort object according to our criteria. The majority were items of pram or cot bedding such as blankets or eiderdowns but they also included a few soft toys, and idiosyncratic objects such as 'big thing', which was an adult pillow covered with ticking and in another case a plastic hammer.

It is possible that dummies and comfort objects fulfil the same function. If this were the case, children who had dummies would be less likely to have comfort objects. The numbers of children who used either one or both objects were compared, but the data did not vary from the expected frequencies. Therefore, children who used a dummy were not less likely to use a comfort object or vice versa.

C Toilet training

All the children were toilet trained during the day, but some were not dry throughout the night. Rather than ask the parents directly if their child was dry in the night, observers recorded if the child was still put to bed in a nappy. This assessment assumes that nappy wearing reflects lack of bladder or bowel control. Ten per cent of the children were still wearing a nappy at night, most of them in the 3–3½ age band and more of them middle class than working class. Significantly more of them were boys, 13 boys to 3 girls ($\chi^2 = 6.8$; d.f.1; $P < 0.005$).

Only casual and anecdotal evidence is available on the mothers' attitudes to their children still wearing nappies at night. It seemed to be generally one of unconcern. The only mother who did show concern about the topic had a child who suffered from chronic constipation and her concern was with the physical condition which was causing the child to dirty his nappy at night.

Usually, training the child to use the lavatory is seem as the next step after potty training. A few children in the sample were using a potty only; some were using both the lavatory and a potty, but the majority were using the lavatory all the time. Observers noted which was used during the observations. Almost all the 4–4½-year-olds had stopped using a potty (see Table 4.1).

Table 4.1 Percentages of children using lavatories as opposed to potties by age

	Pot only	Both Pot and Lavatory	Lavatory only
	%	%	%
3–3½ yrs	3	9	26
3½–4 yrs	1	8	26
4–4½ yrs	0	1	28

D Washing and bathing

Over half the children were not observed taking a bath, 22 per cent of these were middle class, 34 per cent working class. We distinguished bathing from washing by stipulating that bathing had to included body immersion at some point in the proceedings. Eleven per cent of the parents chose not to use the bath for this purpose and this included only one child whose family did not have a fixed bath. Most of these children were bathed in the kitchen sink, but people also used a zinc bath, baby baths and washing up bowls.

E. Food and concern over eating

The majority of families ate their main meal in the evening. It was usually (except in hot weather) a cooked meal including meat or fish and vegetables. Often the vegetables were tinned or frozen and potato chips were very popular. This was frequently followed by a simple sweet course, such as jelly, blancmange, rice pudding or a shop bought cake. Breakfast generally consisted of cereal followed by toast or the latter on its own. In exceptional cases, a cooked breakfast was eaten, such as boiled egg or bacon sandwich. Fruit juice, milk, milk shakes, coffee and tea were drunk during the day and with meals. A midday meal often consisted of sandwiches, beans on toast or a local speciality, grilled oatcakes with bacon and cheese.

Table 4.2 gives a typical example. It is the diet of a joiner's son aged three years, three months. His diet sheet is from a total of 12 hours' observation, in six two-hour sessions, covering the subject's entire waking day. Each session was on a different day and therefore one whole day is pieced together with information from six separate days.

Eleven per cent of the mothers considered that their child had problems with eating. This was assessed by the observers as being the case if the mother frequently raised the matter with the observer, asking the latter's advice or opinion or mentioned that they had taken the child to the doctor because of their concern with his eating. In one case the mother's anxiety was that the child was overweight and ate too much while in the others it was because they feared that the children were not eating enough. The latter cases included a child who suffered from chronic constipation. This mother had been advised to persuade him to eat foods high in roughage but, in his mother's opinion, he refused to eat a sufficient amount if she attempted this because he had strong food preferences. In all cases except this last one, the children were observed to eat an adequate diet in the observer's estimation. A sub-sample of the main sample participated in a research project examining calorific intake, conducted by Mary Griffiths of the London School of Hygiene and Tropical Medicine. These mothers kept diaries of their children's food intake over a week. They also kept a duplicate portion of food actually consumed by their children and this was later assessed for calorific value. This sub-sample included a number of

Table 4.2   Example of one subject's diet sheet

Time Child Commenced Eating or Drinking	Items
8-06	Weetabix, sugar & milk
8-29.5	Drink of milk (1)
9-44.5	Biscuit (1)
9-49	Biscuit (2)
9-52.5	Drink of milk (2)
10-24.5	Biscuit (3)
11-12.5	Sweet (1)
11-39.5	Sweet (2)
12-07	Sweet (3)
13-00	Banana Sandwich Drink of milk (3)
14-31	Stick of celery
14-40.5	Drink of milk (4)
15-02	Drink of water
17-15	Shepherd's pie, peas
17-57.5	Drink of orange squash
18-46.5	Drink of milk (5)
19-55	Drink of milk (6)

children whose mothers had felt they were eating inadequately. Mary Griffiths considered that all the children were eating sufficient for their needs. A common reaction of the mothers after completing their diaries was amazement at the amount of food their children were in fact eating. Frequently, for instance, they had been unaware of the amount of milk that their children were drinking.

Eating problems, perceived by mothers, did show a tendency to decline with age. Of the 11 per cent of the children who were considered to have eating problems, 7 per cent were in the 3–3½ age band, 4 per cent in the 3½–4 year group and only 1 per cent in the oldest group. There was also a tendency for working class mothers (9 per cent of the children were working class, 2 per cent middle class), rather than middle class mothers, to perceive their children as having this problem.

In only one exceptional case did an observer consider a child was receiving an inadequate diet. This was not one of the children whose parents had expressed concern. This was again a child who had been observed for 12 hours and the observer felt that she had recorded a valid sample day's diet for the child. She was woken for breakfast with a packet of potato crisps and went through the day having a series of snacks: a jam sandwich; a packet of sweet cigarettes; a fancy cake; tea with lots of sugar lumps; more sugar lumps on their own; a rusk crushed and moistened with Ostermilk; and occasional sips of milk out of the milk bottle which she sneaked from the pantry to her mother's displeasure.

Snacks of biscuits, sweets, ice-pops, ice-creams and lollies were eaten frequently between meals by the majority of children. A few parents had a policy of offering raw vegetables and fruit as snacks and a few provided the child with his day's sweet ration during the morning leaving it to the child to eat them all immediately or save some for later in the day. The majority of children were given snacks when they asked the parents for them and were always bought sweets when they accompanied their parents out shopping or passed a sweet shop on the way, for instance, to collect an older sibling from school. There was a tendency for the working class children to spend more time eating snacks than the middle class children.

F The social aspects of meals times

Meal times can provide an opportunity for a child to talk and interact with his parents. We thought it would be interesting to assess how many children in the sample were offered this opportunity. Initially, we considered the simple category of 'sitting round a table while eating' would suffice. It became evident during the pilot study that the majority of families were likely to assemble informally for meals, sitting in armchairs with a tray on their laps, or using television tables pulled up to their chairs or standing round a breakfast bar. All these gatherings might still provide the social situation in which we were interested and we therefore defined a check-list category, 'Dining'. 'Dining' may be defined by actual eating or by the individuals concerned assembling in a specific situation before eating, or remaining there during or after eating. Further rules, given in Appendix 1, governed precisely whether another individual was dining with the child.

The majority of the sample had a specific place to sit for some or all of their meals. This is more a middle class tendency than a working class one. Less than half the subjects took part in this activity when it constituted a family gathering. Sometimes a child sat at the kitchen table alone or with his brothers and sisters while the parents or mother, if it was a midday meal, took theirs into the sitting room (see Table 4.3). In a few families the father came home later in the evening and ate his meal separately. In several cases where this was the arrangement, the mother ate neither with the children nor with her husband and appeared only to eat pickings while she was cooking and scraps when she cleared up after the meals. Frequently the children who did not sit down at a set place were eating sandwiches or food from plastic bowls. They wandered about the living room or kitchen, or sat on the floor to eat while watching television.

Table 4.3   Percentage of children dining with or without adult company

Class	Dining Observed	No Dining Observed	χ^2	Level of Signif.
Middle	83	17		
			4.39	NS
Working	67	33		

Class	Dining Observed with Adult	No Dining Observed with Adult	χ^2	Level of Signif.
Middle	58	42		
			7.89	$P<0.005$
Working	35	65		

G Sleep, bedtime and associated problems

Parents reported that their children slept a twelve hour night (mean 12.03; SD 0.85). There were no differences between groups. Parents also reported that no child in the sample still had a regular nap during the day, although some of the children did drop off to sleep occasionally in the course of the day. A number of the children slept during part of an observation period. In some cases they woke up in the morning later than their mothers had predicted, in others they needed to go to bed earlier than usual and some dropped off for a nap during the day. There was no variation in this between groups.

Primarily to help plan observation times, parents were asked when the children got up in the morning and when they went to bed. Getting up included actually coming downstairs as opposed to being awake in their own beds or possibly snuggling in with their parents. The times show quite a wide variation, peaking at 8.30 in the morning, but there were no consistent group variations. Similar variation was shown with bedtimes, with a peak at 20 –20 hours; again there was no group difference, (see Table 4.4).

When asking parents when their children went to bed, we found this was not always a clear-cut issue. Most, but not all, children were put to bed and left to go off to sleep on their own. Other children often dropped off to sleep in the living room and then were carried to bed, asleep, by their parents. A number of these children were not carried up until their parents went to bed, which accounts for most of the later bedtimes. The reverse occurred with one child, a four-year-old, who required very little sleep. His mother reported his bedtime as 11.30pm in the initial interview but subsequently explained that it was often later. Frequently, he was left by his parents to potter about downstairs on his own, playing and watching television, after they had gone to bed. He would come up by himself, usually when the television closed down, and pat them to wake up so that they could tuck him into bed. A few children needed parents to stay with them until they went to sleep, for what, in some cases, the parents felt to be an excessively long time. In one extreme case, the child insisted that the mother actually went to bed at the same time as she did. The father was a policeman. He was out on shiftwork for a fair proportion of the evenings. The mother actually had to get undressed and into the twin bed in her daughter's room and pretend to got to sleep. When the father was out, she ended up

Table 4.4 Children's rising and bedtimes

	Times (to nearest .5 hr)	% of children
Rising	6-30	1
	7-30	15
	8-00	13
	8-30	40
	9-00	13
	9-30	13
	10-00	4
	10-30	1
Bedtime	18-30	2
	19-00	2
	19-30	16
	20-00	15
	20-30	35
	21-00	12
	21-30	11
	22-00	4
	23-00	1
	23-30	1

going to bed at 8.30pm with her daughter, and spending the night in the twin bed. In another household, there were no beds for the children and so they spent the entire night on the settees in the living room. Another sleep problem which beset a few parents was when the child refused to stay in his own bed throughout the night and persisted in coming into their bed.

Observers assessed whether parents perceived either of these two areas as a problem. If parents discussed the matter with the observer and were seeking ways of changing the child's behaviour or if they described the situation as seriously interfering with their own domestic lives, it was scored as a problem. More children gave difficulty going off to sleep than in getting out of their beds in the night. A very small number of children presented their parents with both of these problems (see Table 4.5). Seventy-nine per cent of the children who gave rise to the first problem were working class; the social class difference is just not significant at the 0.01 level.

Table 4.5   Percentage of children considered by parents to have sleep problems

	Stays in own bed %	Will not stay in own bed %
Goes off to sleep easily	86	2
Will not go off to sleep easily	8	4

H Parental supervision

We thought it would be interesting to assess whether children were allowed beyond the curtilage of the parental home, using curtilage in the legal sense. In other words, was the child allowed to go unaccompanied into public areas beyond the garden, yard or drive of his own home, or step out of the front door into the pavement or street where for example, a terraced house was concerned? This was assessed by the observer both in terms of the child's observed behaviour and also from anecdotes reported by parents or references arising in the course of conversation between the parent and the child. Given that the vast majority of children did have access to some outdoor play space, this seemed an interesting point for comparison across the children. This limitation showed no change with age: 54 per cent of the children were allowed out and 46 per cent were not. Neither did this tie in with the busyness of the immediate street, nor show any class or sex differences. A large number of those who were allowed out had closely circumscribed points beyond which they were not allowed to pass: for example, as far as a particular lamp post on one side of the home and the letter box on the other, while parents frequently monitored the child's whereabouts and tapped on the window or shouted if he over-stepped the prescribed limits.

Often parents were in a dilemma because they would have preferred their child not to play outside their home boundaries but other children in the neighbourhood were doing so. Either they had to enforce a rule to the effect that their child remained in their garden or yard, which meant that neighbouring children who were playing outside were unavailable to him, or they had to overcome their anxiety and let him play beyond their boundaries. Sometimes the neighbouring children were slightly older than their child and so, in order that he could play with them, the parents had allowed the child his freedom when he was younger than they would have wished. This could operate in reverse. For example, one child in the pilot study who lived in a terraced house was allowed on the 'front' but the immediately neighbouring children were not. Consequently his sole contact with other children was through the crack under their yard gate and a great deal of time was spent pushing objects of mutual interest through the crack. The observer never saw the other children at all in the entire course of observation.

In some terraced streets there seemed to be an excellent mutual monitoring service. A little boy played on his 'front' and then crossed over the street and was wandering up and down the opposite side. A passing woman peered at the observer and said 'Is he with you?'. The observer was concentrating on her recording and was slow in answering. The woman turned back to the child, told him off for being across the street and saw him back across the road to his 'home' side.

One child did give an observer concern and reflected the occasional over-estimation of young children's understanding shown by a few parents. The family lived in a quiet terraced street but their home was only 50 yards from a very busy main road at the bottom of the street. The child was three years, two months old and was allowed the use of the street but frequently went into the main road. The observer wished to let the mother know that the child was doing this. However, when she managed to introduce the subject the mother showed that she was fully aware by saying that the child's best friend had been killed there a couple of months earlier, which she would have thought would have stopped him going down to the main road.

The open nature of new housing estates can give rise to problems when parents know that their child is unwelcome in a neighbour's house or garden where he is continually attracted by the neighbour's children. One mother found this situation with an adjacent neighbour acutely embarrassing, and resorted to taking her daughter for long walks to avoid bother with her about going round to the neighbour's. On the other hand, a few parents seemed insensitive to their neighbour's attitudes to the visits of their children. One little girl in a new small private housing estate persistently called at various houses and was frequently rejected in very firm tones. On several occasions she was allowed in briefly and the observer (after a brief explanation of the study, neighbours were very accommodating in allowing the observer in as well) was amazed at the acerbity of the neighbours and that the child still wished to visit. For example, her remarks were either ignored or answered sharply, as in: Child (noticing Wimbledon on the television) conversationally, 'I don't like tennis'. Neighbour, shortly, 'Well that's too bad, isn't it; it's not your TV.'

Similarly, a few parents found a persistent small visitor a nuisance. By and large, most parents seemed tolerant of their own and other people's children's visits and excursions. A few families lived in small cul-de-sacs where all the families seemed to have children. This appeared to work very well with a wide age range of children mixing and playing at times together. No family objected to balls and missiles being thrown about and the occasional father who appeared in the evenings to play with his own children ended up organising games involving all the children.

While the formal rule of whether the child was permitted to go beyond his home boundaries did not show a variation with the child's age, another measure that we took did. This was a detailed observed recording on the check-list of what proportion of the working day was spent by the child not 'under the eye' of his mother or other caretaker figure; we defined this as when the child was 'Out of the same room and out of sight of parents or caretaker'. Thus, this was not scored if both the child and his mother were, for instance, in the living room and he was hidden behind the sofa, or if he moved into the hall but was still visible to his mother. It was scored if he moved out of sight into another room. Similarly, if he was playing outside, this would not be recorded while the caretaker was watching from the window, but would be scored when no-one was watching or the child was out of view from a window. The three to three and a half-year-olds spent 74 per cent of their time under a caretaker's eye; this decreased with age to 67 per cent. Youngest children spend the least time, 65 per cent, the Only children most, 74 per cent. Neither the difference across age groups or family positions is significant at the .01 level.

I Discipline, control and misbehaviour

Parents differed widely in what they considered to be socially acceptable behaviour from their children. Some parents were prepared to tolerate aspects of their children's behaviour which other parents would find totally unacceptable. This tolerance varied both with events leading to damage and disruption in the home and to concern with behaviour likely to cause injury to the child himself or to another child. For example, one mother walked into her bedroom to find her three and a half-year-old daughter, five-year-old son and two other children leaping from the top of the wardrobe on to their parents' double bed, having pulled all the bedclothes off to clear the way. The mother smiled and commented: 'I'll have to see to the bed when you've all finished'. In contrast, another mother insisted that her small son pack up and return to the toy cupboard any toy with which he had been playing before he fetched another. Some children were not allowed access to any potentially harmful objects such as knives, scissors and electric points, while another child regularly leant into the stove and stirred the embers with a poker, without the mother commenting. However, both the child permitted to lay waste the parents' bedroom and the one who was allowed to stir the fire, were smacked and severely told off for swearing, which their parents obviously considered was intolerable behaviour in a young child.

On a few occasions children were seen to behave differently when they were or were not 'under the parental eye'. One girl discreetly departed into the best 'front' sitting room while her mother was busy in the kitchen, climbed on to the back of an armchair and from there on to the mantelpiece, and spent some time examining the fragile glass ornaments kept there. At a later date the observer learnt from the mother that these ornaments were strictly 'out of bounds' to the child. Similarly, a four-year-old boy, who was looked after every/day by his grandmother, was playing on the kitchen floor with some marbles. The grandmother finished washing up the breakfast things, announced that she was going upstairs to make the beds and left. The child immediately opened a cupboard door, inside which were gold stemmed champagne glasses; he dropped his marbles into the glasses and whirled them around inside. Eventually, footsteps were heard coming downstairs and before his grandmother came into the kitchen every glass was back in the cupboard and the child was again innocently rolling his marbles in front of the cupboard.

More serious incidents also occurred occasionally. One little girl, when her mother was not watching, repeatedly teased, mauled and pinched a large, boisterous puppy which the family had recently acquired. Eventually, the dog would snap at the child's fingers and she would burst into tears, then run to her mother, crying that the dog had bitten her. The dog was then severely punished. A four-year-old boy repeatedly taunted his two-year-old brother who would become enraged and finally, if he managed to catch his older brother, bite him. The older child would rush to his mother and display the wound. This mother was very concerned about the younger child's habit of biting and did punish him when it happened, but had her suspicions as to why it was happening. In another case, the reverse seemed to occur. A four-year-old girl was extremely jealous of her new baby brother; in her mother's presence she attempted to slap pieces of plasticine on the baby's head, pull and pinch his cheeks and grab at his hands and feet. While the mother was concerned not to acerbate the situation by betraying her lack of trust in the older child, she was frightened of leaving the girl alone with the baby. However, when the mother was out of the room, the child stopped molesting the baby and behaved affectionately towards him.

While parents had been told that the observer was not going to interfere with the child's behaviour unless the child was going to hurt himself or someone else, there were a few occasions when this posed a dilemma. One instance was when a brother, the subject and some neighbourhood friends assembled in the parents' bedroom and were pouring water and talcum powder into the parents' bed and generally creating havoc. The parents were extremely house-proud and the observer felt that she would be unwelcome for another observation if they were not informed of what was going on upstairs. However, the observer had to be careful that her own standards did not intrude. For example, in the pilot study, a little girl was taking rides on the back of her friend's chopper bike. They were hurtling down a very steep cobbled bank and she was holding on precariously to the other child's jersey while both of them were screaming with laughter and a nasty accident seemed imminent. The observer drew the mother's attention to what was happening and the mother came out, saw what her daughter was doing, and half-heartedly told her to stop. The children continued and the mother laughed and turned to the observer, saying 'I've told her about it before', leaving the observer with the impression that it was a frequent occurrence and she should not have interfered.

Most children were well behaved and successfully controlled by their parents. Occasional flare-ups were precipitated by property disputes between sibling and friends, refusals to eat at meal times and summons from a parent to come into the house for a meal or bedtime when the child was out playing with his friends. Particularly if the child was hungry or tired, a temper tantrum would result. Parents, in general conversation with the observers, suggested that the frequency of temper tantrums was declining with the children's ages. Whereas parents ruefully described times when their children had caused them acute embarrassment by throwing a temper tantrum in public, out shopping for instance, these incidents were now a thing of the past. We recorded the behaviour as a temper tantrum if at least one or some of the following occurred: muscular rigidity; breath held; repeated violent limb movements; body hurled on to the floor; head banging; shouting and screaming; objects hurled. Twenty-nine per cent of the children were observed to have at least one temper tantrum in the course of observation. The incidence of temper tantrums declined significantly with age (see Table 4.6).

Table 4.6 Percentage of children observed to have temper tantrums

Age	Temper Tantrum %	No Temper Tantrum %
3–3½ yrs	13	24
3½–4 yrs	13	21
4–4½ yrs	3	26

$\chi^2 = 11.07$ $P < 0.005$

Physical punishment from parents to attempt to stop a temper tantrum was not seen, although frequently being smacked and told off was the precipitating event. Parents used both verbal and physical punishment to control their children. This verbal aspect of the parents' and the children's behaviour will be discussed in the chapter on language. Thirty-eight per cent of the children were smacked by their parents in the course of observation; in the majority of cases the mother did the smacking. In all cases the parents used their hands and a single smack was involved. One child was threatened with a cane in a way which implied that he was beaten with it on some occasions. A small number of children were physically restrained by their parents as a punishment. In one case a child was thrown with considerable force by the mother onto a settee, in a way which caused the observer severe concern. This followed a series of episodes when the child had been smacked and then finally tried to hide from her mother behind the observer, when she was dragged out and thrown on to the settee. The child had virtually no toys and was confined the whole time to the sitting room where she spend most of her time running wildly around the room hurling the chairs over and screaming. Her family made no attempt to provide her with any activity apart from television watching. Her behaviour, as a result, was obviously causing considerable strain in the mother and there were also three younger brothers and sisters, all of whom, except for the baby, behaved in the same way. A few of the subjects were punished by being made to go to their bedrooms.

Most parents attempted to distract their children from events which were likely to lead to a confrontation and so divert them before a temper tantrum occurred. 'Options', again discussed in the language chapter, were used in this way. The parents would suggest that the child took part in some activity and so prevent him from committing a misdemeanour.

Disputes between children usually centred round property, one child wanting an object which another child had. For example, two little girls were dressing up and the younger sister, the subject, wanted the only available piece of net curtain which her sister was already wearing as a bridal veil. The dispute was eventually resolved when their grandmother found another piece of net for the younger child. Fifty-four per cent of the children hit another child in the course of a dispute, and thirty-four per cent received a blow. While being hit by other children did not vary with any of the four independent variables, there was a significant effect according to family position, for hitting another child. Eldest children did most hitting, Only children least.

Table 4.7   Percentage of children who hit another child

Family Position	Hit Another Child %	Did Not Hit Another Child %
Eldest	31	10
Only	8	20
Youngest	16	16

$\chi^2 = 27.27$ $P<0.001$

Weeping, regardless of cause was recorded in one category. This declined significantly with age.

Table 4.8   Mean number of intervals in which children wept

Age	Mean Number of Intervals	F Ratio	Level of Significance
3–3½ yrs	7		
3½–4 yrs	4	6.14	$P<0.005$
4–4½ yrs	2		

Laughter, on the other hand, varied with family position, Eldest children laughing least.

Table 4.9   Mean number of intervals in which children laughed

Age	Mean Number of Intervals	F Ratio	Level of Significance
Eldest	36		
Only	45	4.89	$P<0.01$
Youngest	46		

J Affection and dependency

Without exception, the parents delighted in their children. The overwhelming impression was that the parents were immensely proud of their children and considered their accomplishments as 'special' and remarkable. This is not to say that all the parents were perfect. In a few case parents spent very little time with their children, but all parents gave the impression of the intention of doing their best for their children. For example, one child, the youngest of three, received very little attention from her parents as did her older brother and sister. The mother considered, however, that expensive toys and clothes were of paramount importance to her children. Until immediately before the study started the mother had been working full time in a pottery factory. She had not intended to go back to work until the last child went off to school, but the previous Christmas she had got heavily into debt over the children's presents. Each child had had to have as much spent on him as the others. The boy received a new bicycle and the girls a doll's pram apiece, the most luxurious the observer had ever seen. To pay off the debt the mother had got a job and paid the next door neighbour (who was not a registered childminder) to look after the youngest. She described the neighbour as 'as thick as a plank' and the observer's incidental observations of the neighbour suggested that the woman was not an ideal childminder. Yet the mother intended to return again to what she herself saw as inadequate care for her child, in order to provide the children with expensive presents the following Christmas.

Affectionate physical contact ranged widely between families. Eight per cent of the children were never observed being cuddled, hugged or sitting on a parent's lap. Kissing seemed to be mainly reserved for formal, symbolic occasions or farewell. Fathers would often ask for a kiss on return from work or children were expected to give and receive a kiss on the way to bed. Forty-one per cent of the children gave kisses and 53 per cent received a kiss. Neither cuddling nor kissing showed variation with the independent variables. Social games such as tickling and play wrestling are discussed in the next chapter. 'Functional' physical contact was also recorded, i.e. when a child was held to have his face washed, shoes put on or to cross a busy road, Similarly, this did not vary between groups.

Partings from parents or other members of the family were still an occasion for distress with some of the children. A few fathers would

slip discreetly off to work without the child seeing in order to preclude tears. With some parents, this aspect affected their attitudes
towards Play Group or Nursery School attendance and this is discussed in Chapter 9.

Discussion and conclusions

Interest in thumb and finger sucking and dummy use has been
inspired by both psychoanalytic theory and the potential relationship between persistent sucking habits and malocclusion, for example buck teeth. Data on sucking in older children have mainly been
gathered from parental interviews. Klackenberg (1949) found that
thumb sucking decreased gradually from 47 per cent at two years to
21 per cent at age six. Traisman and Traisman (1958) report that the
average age at which thumb sucking ceased in a large sample of children was three to eight years. Our data agree with these findings, in
that the decline in thumb sucking is gradual betweem the ages of
three to four and a half years. While diverse findings have been
reported on the relationship between early infant feeding styles and
later thumb sucking, Traisman *et al.*, considered that thumb sucking
took over from dummy sucking when the dummy was withdrawn.
The Newsons (1968) also thought this accounted for the class difference in thumb sucking when they found in their study of four-year-
olds. They concluded that social pressure encouraged middle class
parents to remove dummies from their children earlier than they
were removed from the working class children and as a result there
was more persistent thumb sucking among the middle class class
subjects in their sample. Probably, changes in social outlook
account for the lack of class difference in dummy use in the present
study. Our finding, that children who use a dummy sucked their
thumbs as much as children who did not use a dummy, may be
explained by partial dummy removal, in that many children were
restricted to particular times when they were allowed their dummies
and compensated by increased thumb sucking in the intervening
periods. Our measurement of total time spent thumb sucking is
probably an underestimate, as this behaviour is most likely to occur
immediately the child wakes and before he finally drops off to sleep,
the periods most likely to be under-represented by the observation
schedules.

Far fewer children in this study were observed to use a comfort object than the number reported to the Newsons, 10 per cent as opposed to 31 per cent. We suspect this may be a function of mis-reporting on the part of the parents despite the Newsons' prompt: 'Would he make a fuss if you couldn't find it one night?'. Several parents volunteered the information that their child was very dependent on a particular object and gave accounts of family hunts at bedtime to find the beloved object. When it had not been seen throughout the course of observation, the observer commented that the particular object had not been in evidence and in these cases it was eventually located. Usually it had been stuffed into the bottom of the toy box or a cupboard, where it had obviously lain for a while, suggesting that the parents had not noticed that a habit they took for granted had now ceased.

The Newsons found that more working than middle class children were still wetting their beds, at least occasionally, at four years of age. The measure we used to indicate bladder or bowel control, that the child wore a nappy at night, may not be directly comparable to their data. Anecdotal evidence suggested that several children, although out of nappies, still had occasional accidents at night. Our measure was chosen as a reliable observational measure, but is an underestimation of the total number of children who were still not totally toilet trained at night. Perhaps again, the fact that more mid-dle class children are still wearing nappies at night and that the pre-vailing attitude was one of unconcern about toilet training is a reflection of changing attitudes.

Similarly, mothers were tolerant in allowing children to continue to use a potty rather than a lavatory. Potties have the advantage, to the child, of being potentially available in a warm place, such as in front of the sitting room fire or in the kitchen. Their use also means that the child does not have to isolate himself from the general social situation by trudging up the stairs or 'out the back'. The prevailing attitude seemed to be that it was important to get the child used to using a lavatory before he went to Nursery or Infant School – where he would have to use one.

The variation according to the social class of children observed to take a bath suggests that a daily bath is still largely a middle class practice. However, an appreciable number of both classes chose not to use the family bath for bathing their children. One obvious disad-vantage to a full bath is that it takes more hot water than a baby bath or washing up bowl. However, other considerations were also important. A child can be bathed in a receptacle in a warm kitchen or in front of the living room fire. Often bath time coincided with the time when the mother was busy cooking the evening meal and the child was under her eye, playing happily in the water, whilst she alternated between washing him and tending the cooker.

A major cause of parental anxiety seems to be unnecessary concern that the child is eating an insufficient amount of food. Given the experience of parents' relief when they keep records of the child's actual intake and that a wide social range of mothers were capable of doing this, it might well be helpful for family doctors or Health Visitors, when parents seek their advice, to suggest that the latter keep a simple diary.

A small number of working class parents considered that an important function of Nursery School was to teach their children manners, in particular table manners. Given that so many families do not have meals in a traditional, formal setting, it is likely that quite a few children will have had little experience of sitting this way for meals before they get to school and puts the parents' attitude to the function of Nursery School in perspective, a point teachers might bear in mind.

The number of children who were not put to bed and left to go to sleep on their own, in a conventional fashion, is surprising and seems to reflect the current ethos of tolerance in childrearing practice. Several parents who perceived their child's sleeping habits as posing problems regretted that they had not taken a firmer stand earlier. They found it impossible to change the child's habit of having to go to sleep downstairs and then to be carried up to bed, or of having them stay with the child till he went to sleep. Impossible that is, in that a tough line meant shouting and crying from the child, and they were very conscious that this would be overheard and would disturb their neighbours, a pressing problem in terraced and semi-detached housing. Also, where there were other children in the family, either older or younger, they also would be disturbed. Some parents felt quite desperate about the situation, particularly when their own sleep was disrupted by the child coming into their bed during the night and again they were convinced that if they had foreseen how things were going to develop then they would never have permitted the habit to start.

Monitoring where the child went on his own varied widely with individual families and did not show the class difference we had anticipated, i.e. that working class children would be permitted to wander further afield on their own. The lack of differential control over boys and girls at this age accords with the Newsons' findings with their study of children at four years of age (1968), where parents were not restricting the movements of one sex more than the other, in contrast to their later report on the children at seven years (1976). By then parents were taking greater care over accompanying their daughters, as opposed to their sons, on ventures outside the home. The authors attributed this development to parents' fears about the greater risk of molestation for little girls.

The close proximity of other families with different standards poses a variety of problems to urban parents, both street and estate dwellers. It is difficult to enforce a rule with a child when his neighbourhood friends are not bound by it. One family lived in a newly built cul de sac of half a dozen houses, one house still being unoccupied. Their son spent most of the time playing with the children from the two adjacent houses and they repeatedly all gathered in the back garden of the unoccupied house and attempted to pull down a newly erected fence to make 'a house'. The boy's mother retrieved her son three times and soundly told him off for going into the garden. The other parents ignored what their children were doing and finally the poor child stood at the corner of the plot, watching the other children play and silently shaking his head when they persistently called to him to join them.

While 38 per cent of the parents were observed to smack their children, this figure gives no guide to the proportion of families prepared to use smacking as a punishment. The majority of children gave little occasion for severe punishment and probably a much higher number of parents did smack their children very occasionally. The majority of children were cheerful and amenable and, as has been mentioned, all the parents saw themselves as proud of and interested in their children. It is this very deep reserve of good will and interest which has been tapped by various action research programmes, such as the Red House Project (Poulton and James, 1975) and could be utilised more by the teaching profession to forge the initial link between the home and the educational system.

Chapter 5
The children's activities and the toys and equipment available to them

A major part of the study was to describe the activities in which the children took part, who participated with the children in these activities, what toys and equipment were available to the children and how these aspects of their lives related to the independent variables. The term 'activity' is used to avoid labelling the children's behaviour in terms of playfulness and activities involving domestic tasks will be included, such as washing-up or dusting, as well as conventional children's 'play' activities like tricycle riding and building with blocks. Only the 'functional' categories discussed in the last chapter are excluded.

We set out to record who initiated activites: whether for instance the child himself started doing a jigsaw puzzle or whether the activity was suggested by the mother. However we found in the pilot study that this was impossible with pencil and paper check-list recording techniques, where an assessment of the behaviour is made concurrently with the behaviour itself, as social interaction in the home between a child of this age and his family is a fluid, subtle and dynamic process. It was therefore impossible to define validly and reliably the point when a particular social interaction, geared to a specific activity, had begun. This would only have been feasible with video recording where 'post hoc' analysis is possible. Similarly, we found it impossible to make reliable assessments which reflected different levels of intimacy of social involvement such as parallel and co-operative activity and so restricted ourselves to one measure of social participation. Activities were recorded as 'joint activities' with another individual if one of the following criteria was fulfilled: the participants' attention was deployed on that activity for the preponderant length of the time interval; speech from the other individual to the subject about the activity was continuous and contained more than one concept; two or more statements were addressed to the subject relevant to the activity during the time interval; brief non-verbal communication concerning the child's activity had to occur more than once, or once with a spoken statement.

Initially we had assumed we could quantify the toys and equipment available to the child by counting the number of toys he possessed. However, from our pilot study experience we found this to be impracticable. If an observer counted the child's toys before observation commenced, it biased the parents' behaviour into directing the child's activities to his toys. If they were counted after observation the parents were frequently concerned that the child had not played with his toys in 'the right way'. Another problem was that toys were often spread throughout the house rather than being easily available for counting. In addition, the existence of a particular toy in the household did not necessarily mean that it was available to the child. We saw, for instance, prestigious dolls kept permanently in cellophane on the mantelpiece, or toys stored in places inaccessible to the child. We also found in the pilot study that children passed relatively little of their time in activities with commercial toys, more was spent in using general household items. Any 'toy count' would not include these items and would give an invalid picture of the objects and equipment available to the child. We therefore recorded at the end of the time interval all items used by children in their activities. Items were only recorded once and not included if used solely in 'functional' activities. We considered that this recording method gave a valid picture, given the extensive observation time per child, of the toys and equipment genuinely available to him.

Inevitably the types of toys and domestic equipment that the children used in their activities were very varied. To produce a meaningful quantification it was essential to devise toy categories which were as far as possible homogeneous in terms of the experience the toy or item could potentially provide for the child. Toy categories were also designed to reflect the behaviour category system: for example, there is a behaviour category 'Arrange and Shape' and also a toy category 'Arrange and Shape Toys'. However, contrary to the behaviour coding, the toys are classified according to their conventional use: for example, if a child was using books as 'stepping stones' on the floor, the behaviour would be recorded as spontaneous

Table 5.1 **Activities ranked in order of pecentage of children who engaged in each activity**

Reference for Full Category Definition (see Appendix I)	Activity	% of Children Engaging in Activity	Mean % of Waking Day Spent in Activity
26 P	Watching other people	100	6
15 L	Spontaneous running and jumping	100	6
17	Representational fantasy play	99	8
10±	Combined visual and tactile object examination	99	3
23 F	Running errands	98	1
12 P	Preparation for a future or current activity	98	1
26 I	Watching inanimate objects	96	2
14 F	Climbing, swinging and bouncing	95	3
8 L	Looking at books	94	3
11 M	Mobility and unspecific attention	94	2
11 I	Immobile with vacuous gaze	94	<1
18/19/20	Complex fantasy	93	3
2 T	Television	92	9
25 M	Miniature social play	91	1
13 M	Miniature physical activities	91	1
15 T	Walking or running according to restraint of another individual	89	3
12 S	Sorting, searching and rummaging	86	1
15 V	Toy vehicle riding and driving	79	4
7 N	Noise-making activities	78	1
34 S	Showing items to another person	77	<1
3 D	Water play	76	2
9 A	Activities with animals	75	1
26 W	Looking out of window	72	1
14 P	Pushing and pulling large toys and objects	72	1

Table 5.1 cont'd (2)

Reference for Full Category Definition (see Appendix 1)	Activity	% of Children Engaging in Activity	Mean % of Waking Day Spent in Activity
5 F	Cutting, sticking, folding and glueing	69	1
4 D	Drawing and colouring	68	2
15 B	Rolling about	67	<1
25 G	Gross physical social play	66	1
16 D	Dressing up	63	<1
13 U	Whirling and waving objects	63	<1
6 C	Construction and piling	60	2
13 B	Ball games and activities	59	1
6 A	Arranging, matching or shape games	57	1
10 F	Fiddling, without tactile exploration while looking at an object	57	1
6 P	Packing or unpacking objects into containers	52	1
9 N	Number activities	50	<1
25 H	Hiding games	47	<1
23 M	General household and garden maintenance	45	1
5 S	String and thread activities	44	<1
3 S	Sand play	41	1
7 F	Finger play and rhyme activities	36	1
11 ±	Automanipulation with visual attention	36	1
5 P	Painting	35	1
8 R	Being read to	29	1
4 M	Soft modelling	24	1
8 L	Letter activities	24	<1
2 R	Listening to radio or records	22	<1
22 G	Game playing	19	3
8 N	Being told stories	15	<1
23 C	Cooking	11	<1
14 O	Being pushed while in a wheeled vehicle or on a swing	10	<1

locomotor activity, but the books would be listed as books in the toy classification. Similarly, domestic items and equipment were classified in terms of their conventional use.

Section 1: The children's activities

The activities under discussion are listed in Table 5.1. They are presented in rank order in terms of the percentage of children who engaged in each activity; the mean time spent in that activity is expressed as the percentage of the children's mean waking day.

A Physical activities

All the children in the study spontaneously ran, jumped or skipped at some time during observation. We distinguished between spontaneous locomotor activity on the part of the child and that which was dictated by the demands of another person. For example, if a mother called her child into the house from the garden for a meal and he ran in, this was not recorded as spontaneous activity but as 'Travelling'. Middle class children tended to engage in more spontaneous locomotor activity than working class children and Only Children less than Eldest and Youngest. 'Travelling' did not show any variation between groups. We grouped all climbing, swinging and bouncing into one category. This mainly occurred on furniture in the house, climbing up the banisters, bouncing on settees and beds, swinging on doors and gates. Again, Only children tend to do less than the other two groups. While girls tended to engage in both spontaneous locomotor activity and the climbing, swinging and bouncing category more than boys. Often, while watching television or between bouts of some activity the child was doing while sitting on the floor, he would roll on the ground. This happened sufficiently frequently in the pilot study for us to decide to record it as a separate category and we found it tended to decline with age.

A few children visited a park or playground during observation and had turns on the large toys there and one or two children had rides in coin operated vehicles found outside some supermarkets. These were infrequent events and we therefore have included this type of equipment under 'Vehicle riding'. Seventy-nine percent of the children took part in this type of activity. There was a tendency for boys to do it more than girls but there was no class difference. In the previous category the child himself had to be propelling the vehicle; we separated this from sitting in the same type of equipment and being propelled by someone else. Only 10 per cent of the children sat and were pushed and this was mainly in garden or park swings. Mothers of Only children tended to participate more in this latter activity and in the 'Vehicle riding' more than mothers of Eldest or Youngest children.

We included under 'Ball play' play with all types of balls, footballs to golf balls, and any throwing, kicking or batting involved. We separated this from what we called 'Miniature skilled physical' play when children rolled marbles or skipped tiddley-winks. The former was mainly an outdoor activity, the latter indoor. When children played ball with adults conventional balls were used, but when they played on their own they also used sticks and pebbles or hurled other toys about. Children also whirled objects round their heads or banged or knocked them together and this we kept within a separate behaviour category. Boys engaged in significantly more 'Ball play' and whirled and waved objects more than the girls. They also tended to go in for more miniature physical play than the girls (see Table 5.2). Fathers were more likely to take part in ball games with sons, than with daughters. Eighteen per cent of the fathers of boys played ball with their sons, compared to 4 per cent who participated with the daughters, ($\chi^2 = 8.7$; d.f. 1; P<0.005).

Table 5.2   Mean number of intervals observed in ball play and related activities

Activity	Sex	Mean No. of Intervals	F Ratio	Level of Significance
Ball Play	m	15	14.2	P<0.001
	f	5		
Miniature Skilled	m	7	5.51	P<0.02
Physical	f	3		
Whirling and	m	4	12.13	P<0.001
Waving Objects	f	2		

B Activities with materials

Both water and sand play are activities readily available at Nursery Schools and Play Groups in conventional sand pits or water troughs. In the home, the situations in which these activities occur are much less conventional. In both categories we extended the definitions to cover unconventional substances, where the substance was essential to the behaviour, i.e. either it was liquid or granular. 'Water play' always occurred at some time when a child was being bathed and it also happened out of doors in puddles and with trapped water in drain lids or, for instance, old paint pots. A few mothers filled basins of water for their children to play with indoors and a few children had paddling pools in the garden in the summer. Interest in water seemed individual, some 'addicts' spending long periods standing on a chair at the kitchen sink. Overall, 'Water play' did not vary with any of the independent variables. 'Sand play' occurred conventionally with the children who had access to sand pits or a pile of builder's sand, but often took the form of digging at the edges of flower beds or in the cracks of pavements. Indoors, biscuit crumbs, flour, breakfast cereals and polystyrene chips were all utilised for crumbling, pouring and sifting. Again, 'Sand play' showed no group variations.

In the pilot study it became evident that children spent an appreciable amount of time in an activity we called 'Packing', which entailed filling containers such as old handbags, bottles, jars or purses with small objects ranging from marbles, bits of paper to dried peas. In the Main Study, 'Packing' was almost always a solitary activity which girls tended to perform more than boys.

Activities involving string or similar materials, knotting, intertying and threading occurred with less than half the children. A few of them had commercial toy items which were designed for this type of activity but the majority used a piece of old string or cotton which they had acquired. This activity showed no variation between groups and again was mainly solitary, as was 'Noise making'. Noise making entailed any noise making with instruments. Although nearly 80 per cent of the sample took part in this at some time, it was generally an activity of short duration and showed no difference between groups.

'Fabric', a category designed to measure activities similar to the collage work in Nursery Schools, comprised any cutting, sticking, folding and glueing of materials. While sixty-eight per cent of the children took part in this activity, many of the incidents were very short, a brief snip with the scissors across a piece of wallpaper or briefly sticking sellotape to a picture. Only in a few families were extensive collage-type activities seen. For example, a mother assisted her daughter to make an Indian headdress using paper feathers. There is a tendency for girls to engage more in collage-type activities than boys. Only 24 per cent of the children engaged in 'Soft modelling' – squeezing, rolling and shaping pliable substances. A very few children used commercial products such as plasticine and Play Doh, and some modelled with clay, sand or soil in the garden. One or two children were given pastry off cuts to mould while their mothers were cooking. 'Soft modelling' did not vary with any of the independent variables.

Middle class children tended to do more 'Arrange and shape' activities than working class children, the difference falling just short of significance at the 0.01 level. This category included conventional activities with jigsaws and mosaics but also making patterns with, for example, playing cards or pieces of coloured paper. This activity was distinguished from 'Construction' where the child was using interlocking or piling components such as Lego, Playplax or domestic items like empty margarine tubs or shoe boxes. There was a tendency for boys to do more construction than girls.

Sixty-eight per cent of the children drew, scribbled or coloured with pencils, biros, felt tips or crayons during observation. In contrast, only thirty-five per cent of the children did any painting and there is a tendency for more of the middle class children to paint than the working class children. Most painting was done with children's paint boxes; a few children had tub paints and some 'painted' with unconventional substances such as toothpaste or tomato sauce.

C Educational activities

The next group of activities all involve pre-reading, writing or number skills. Under 'Looking at books' we included looking at any printed material, this varying from conventional children's books to posters, pictures, commercial toy instruction pamphlets and widely used mail order catalogues. Only 6 per cent of the sample did not take part in this activity during observation. Fewer children, 29 per cent, were read to in the study. This was distinguished from pointing out and discovering the pictures in the printed material at which they were looking. Both these activities were likely to occur at odd times during the day, only a few children having a specific 'bedtime story'; parents, particularly mothers, treated reading and looking at books as an opportunity to sit down between domestic chores and engage in a relatively peaceful activity. In 77 per cent of the cases where children were read to it was the mother who did the reading. 'Being told a story, such as 'Goldilocks and the Three Bears' was a rare event and only 15 per cent of the children were ever told a story. While 'Looking at books' and 'Being told a story' did not vary according to the independent variables, 'Being read to' occurred significantly more often with middle class children than with working class subjects. Fifty-seven per cent of the middle class children were read to, as opposed to 17 per cent of the working class ($\chi^2 = 12.77$; d.f.1; P<0.001).

We categorised separately 'Letter' and 'Number' activities. 'Letter' activities occurred occasionally in conjunction with conventionally designed equipment for letter learning such as flash cards, the Fisher Price Play School and sets of plastic alphabet letters. A number of parents tried to teach the child to write his name with pencil and paper but more often the settings were totally unconventional, such as drawing the child's initials on the wet kitchen floor in the course of washing clothes, or on a misted window pane. Letter activities occurred with only 24 per cent of the children. Fifty per cent of the children took part in 'Number' activities which were rarely toy-based: telling the time with a clock, playing 'Snap', counting sweets or biscuits, comparing the relative value of coins or the ages of children. Neither activity varied significantly with any of the independent variables.

Among all the 'Educational' activities only 'Being read to' shows a variation with social class. Relatively little time was spent in any one of the 'Educational' activities but all children spent at least some time on one individual category. Therefore, combining all the five categories and comparing the amount of time spent according to the independent variables there is a social class difference just short of significance at the 0.01 level, with middle class children spending more time in educational activities (see Table 5.3).

Table 5.3   Mean number of intervals spent in combined educational activities

	Social Class	Mean No. of Intervals	F Ratio	Level of Significance
Combined Educational Activities	M	35	5.30	P<.02
	W	26		

D Watching and touching

A large proportion of children spent time looking out of the window. At times the activity seemed to be an end in itself, at other times children were watching something specific. Where the person or object could be identified, as for instance when the child ran to the window to watch a visitor come up the path to the house or to watch a dustbin lorry crushing up the rubbish, this was recorded as 'Watch person' or 'Watch inanimate object' concurrently with 'Looking out of the window', as appropriate. 'Looking out of the window' did not vary with any of the independent variables. We included in 'Watching inanimate objects' both stationary and moving objects; the objects were various, such as water gushing down a storm drain, aeroplanes in the sky and shop displays. There was a tendency for boys to spend more time in this behaviour than girls and middle class children spent significantly more time at it than the working class children (see Table 5.4).

Table 5.4   Mean number of intervals spent in watching inanimate objects

	Social Class	Mean No. of Intervals	F Ratio	Level of Significance
Watching Inanimate Objects	M	14	6.97	P<.01
	W	10		

We separated 'watching objects without touching them' from the situation when the child both visually and tactually examined an object. Ninety-nine per cent of the children engaged in this activity with a host of different objects. Again this activity varied with social class, but in the reverse direction from purely visual object examination, working class children spending more time in this type of object examination. (See Table 5.5.) The activity also tended to decline steadily across the three age groups, but this effect is just short of significance at the 0.01 level. Two other visual and tactile behaviour categories recorded were 'Fiddling' and 'Automanipulation plus look'. 'Fiddling' involved the child repetitively performing some tactile activity concurrently with visual attention, but with no evidence of tactile exploration, e.g. repeatedly flipping the cap of a bubble tub on its plastic hinge. 'Automanipulation plus look' is self-descriptive and consisted of activities such as poking and peering at a grazed knee or the child's own toenails. Neither of these latter categories varied with the independent variables.

Table 5.5 Mean number of intervals spent in visual examination of inanimate objects and visual and tactile examination of objects

Activity	Social Class	Mean No. of Intervals	F Ratio	Level of Significance
Visual examination	M	14	6.97	
of inanimate object	W	10		$P < .01$
Visual and tactile	M	18	6.83	
object examination	W	22		$P < .01$

E Mobility and immobility

We distinguished two types of behaviour which were intrinsically inactive. 'Mobile' was a category used to describe the behaviour of a child who spent the major portion of a 30 second time interval engaged in no specific activity, physically, manually or visually. 'Immobile' was recorded when the child went into a 'stare', sitting or standing motionless, staring vacantly into space. Coincidentally, 94 per cent of the children indulged in both of these activities. While there is no variation between groups for 'Immobile', the middle class children spent more time 'Mobile' than the working class subjects (see Table 5.6).

Table 5.6   Mean number of intervals spent 'Mobile'

	Social Class	Mean No. of Intervals	F Ratio	Level of Significance
	M	21		
Mobile			6.17	P<.01
	W	14		

F Preparation for activities

If a child was collectiong together items for some future activity, we defined this as 'Preparation'. It was decided not to code this behaviour as the potential future activity because very often the activity was behaviourally unrelated to that future activity, for example, the assembling of items for painting or some representational fantasy play, clearing a table to make space for some intended activity. Often the child would be distracted in the course of these preparations and did not engage in the activity for which he had been preparing. Often preparation led to searching for particular toys or objects which the child needed for the future activity and this searching appeared to become an end in itself, such as rummaging through a toy box or cupboard, and we therefore categorised 'Sorting' or 'Searching' separately. Preparation for future activities occurred evenly across groups, but 'Sorting' steadily increased with age.

G Activities involving animals

This category globally included any activity related to animals, for example, cleaning out the budgerigar's cage, helping feed the rabbits, cuddling or chasing a dog, talking to a cat, and worm or ladybird hunting. 'Animal-involved activities' varied significantly with family position, Eldest children taking part in least, Youngest most (see Table 5.7).

Table 5.7   Mean number of intervals involved with animals

	Family Position	Mean No. of Intervals	F Ratio	Level of Significance
Animal Involved Activities	Eldest	6		
	Only	10	8.28	P<.001
	Youngest	17		

H Dressing up

Dressing up we placed in two categories. In the first category, the child was actively dressing up, putting on the clothes, adjusting them, taking them off. Once the clothes and articles were on, the child frequently wore them for extended periods. For example, a child would wear a cowboy waistcoat or a plastic bead necklace for an entire observation session, and this was coded separately as wearing a dressing up attire. We found that children used commercial dressing up clothes such as toy nurses' uniforms or police helmets, but they also dressed up in miscellaneous jumble, e.g. their parents' clothes, such as their mother's high heeled shoes or their own clothes. We included in the latter clothing which was 'inappropriate to that particular occasion' as when, for instance, a child donned his swimming trucks over his clothes in the middle of winter. The girls spent more time both actively dressing up and wearing dressing up clothes (see Table 5.8).

I Domestic activities

Less than half the children participated in general domestic activities. As this behaviour occurred relatively infrequently, we included under 'Maintenance' both household and garden chores. Most frequently children helped with dusting, polishing or washing-up, but occasionally the jobs were more unusual, such as stripping wallpaper or taking up old lino from the bathroom floor. We specifically kept 'Cooking' as a separate activity as we thought that it was

Table 5.8   Mean number of intervals involved in dressing up

Activity	Sex	Mean No. of Intervals	F Ratio	Level of Significance
Active Dressing up	m	2	14.39	P<.001
	f	4		
Wearing Dressing up Clothes	m	34	8.57	P<.005
	f	65		

a distinctive activity which potentially provided a wide range of experience to children and was likely to occur in every household. We were perhaps influenced by what turned out to be an exceptional family in the pilot study where the mother assisted her 3½-year-old daughter and 2½-year-old son to make chocolate crispies, the children weighing out the ingredients, preparing the cake tins and competently melting the chocolate on the stove. No equivalent incident occurred in the main study. The cooking which was observed consisted of preparing vegetables and, in a few cases, assisting the mother in rolling out pastry and filling tarts or pies with jam. Neither 'Maintenance' nor 'Cooking' varied with any of the independent variables. Another domestic activity which we recorded in a separate category was 'Fetching' or errand running. Frequently, children were employed on simple errands such as fetching a parent's glasses from the bedroom or being sent into the garden to call their father in to tea. All but 2 per cent of the children ran errands of some sort and there was no variation between groups.

J Social activities

These activities are described as social in that the behaviour is dependent on the active participation or at least the presence of another individual. Vigorous physical play, which we called 'Gross physical play', with another individual, such as being whirled around by the arms, thrown up in the air, or vigorous play fighting or wrestling, was engaged in by 66 per cent of the children. There was no sex difference in terms of either the number of boys and girls who took part in this activity or the time spent in it. Twenty-five per cent of the mothers and 21 per cent of the fathers took part in activities of this sort with their children. We also recorded an activity we called 'Miniature social physical play'. This was less physically vigorous. It depended on the social communication in another person's movements or facial expressions and could include the subsidiary use of an object, e.g. two children with spoon handles in their mouths, flapping them up and down and giggling at each other; tickling or being tickled; peeping round a door. Although subjects participated in both these activities as much with adults as with other children, the effect for family position is significant. Only 25 per cent of the Only children engaged in 'Gross physical play' compared to 43 per cent of the Eldest and 56 per cent of the Youngest children ($\chi^2 = 9.27$; d.f. 2; P<0.01). While 91 per cent of all the children took part in 'Miniature social physical play', again Only children were less likely to do so. Figures for participation being 80, 96 and 94 per cent, for Only, Eldest and Youngest children respectively ($\chi^2 = 9.3$; d.f. 2; P<0.01).

A few children had a traditional game they played on the way to bed or when their fathers returned from work. The parent would walk round the room ostentatiously searching for the child, saying loudly, 'I wonder where he can be' while the child crouched partially hidden, giggling in anticipation of being 'found', behind a chair or the curtains. We also included activities involving hiding objects in this category. Hiding did not vary with the independent variables.

Showing an object to another individual was recorded as a behaviour category in its own right. Frequently a child would be engaged in an activity and then fetch his mother to see what he had done, or he would find something he considered of great interest and demand that another child should come and look. Although a big proportion of children, 77 per cent, engaged in this activity it did not vary with the independent variable.

We had anticipated that older children in families would be required to assist smaller brothers and sisters in functional capacities, perhaps helping to hold a baby's bottle or wipe a runny nose. In fact this rarely occurred and only 10 per cent of the sample ever performed this type of social task, and over half these children were in the Eldest group.

All the children spent time watching other people engaged in activities in which the child himself did not participate. The other people varied from the immediate family to outsiders. Roadmen, dustbin men and neighbours gardening were all silently watched. Older children playing on bicycles or grouped round a motor bike were of interest. Parents performing routine chores might be watched for short periods and also when they were working on something more out of the ordinary, such as hanging curtains or mending the car, they were watched for more sustained periods. 'Watching other people' varied with family position, Eldest children spending more time watching other people and Only least time (See Table 5.9).

Table 5.9   Time spent watching other people

	Family Position	Mean No. of Intervals	F Ratio	Level of Significance
Watching Other People	Eldest	51		
	Only	34	8.64	P<0.001
	Youngest	47		

In the pilot study it became clear that in particular circumstances the information concerning the child's behaviour was incomplete in an important way. For example, one little boy had two brothers, one aged thirteen and the other six. The three boys spent a great deal of time playing 'football', which involved taking turns to kick a football at a particular wall of the home. One child kicked and another was goalie. There were stringent local rules concerning scoring, where one stood to kick and what comprised the goal. A great deal of the time was spent waiting for turns or for someone else to retrieve the ball. A check-list recording of the child's behaviour revealed what he was doing in every 30 second interval but gave no measure to indicate the setting and social participation in the entire event. We therefore designed a behaviour category called 'Game playing'. This was recorded when the subject was participating in an activity with other individuals where the subject was obeying rules which governed the activity. The category was recorded concurrently with the particular activity code appropriate to that time interval. In the summer evenings children occasionally joined a large number of children of mixed ages and would play 'He', 'Grandmother's Footsteps' or fantasy games. 'Game playing' was similarly recorded when the child played games such as Ludo or card games like 'Snap' or 'Happy Families'.

Only 19 per cent of the children took part in any game playing. Both adults or other children, or adults and children together, might be involved in the game playing with the subject. Fifteen per cent of the children played games at some time with other children and when this took place, Youngest children were most likely to be the participants. Thirty-three per cent of the Youngest children took part compared with only 4 per cent of the Eldest and 11 per cent of the Only groups ($\chi^2 = 14.83$; d.f. 2; P<0.001).

While some of the individual activities varied between groups in terms of the participation of other individuals, we wished to compare the overall contact or social interaction the children had with their mothers compared with any other type of individual. Only 8 per cent of the day was composed of paternal interactions. Interactions with siblings, where the children had brothers and sisters, occupied 12 per cent of the day and approximately the same amount of time was spent across all the children in interacting and playing with children who were not siblings (see Table 5.10).

Table 5.10   Percentage of the day spent in social interaction with other people

Participating Individuals	Mean % of Day
Mother	40
Father	8
Other adults	7
Siblings (Only children excluded)	12
Other children	11

The amount of maternal interaction did not vary among any of the independent variables. However, paternal interaction showed a significant difference according to family position, Youngest children spending less time than the other two groups in activities engaged in with their fathers. While all the children spent an equivalent amount of time in social interaction with adults *other than* their parents, when parental and other adult time is combined, the total amount of adult interaction time delines with age, and Youngest children receive least adult interaction (see Table 5.11).

Table 5.11 Mean number of intervals spent in social interaction with adults

Participating Individual	Family Position	Mean No. of Intervals	F Ratio	Level of Significance
	Eldest	66		
Father	Only	72	9.66	P<.001
	Youngest	39		
All adults including parents	Eldest	394		
	Only	454	12.95	P<.001
	Youngest	331		
	Age			
All adults including parents	3 - 3½	417		
	3½ - 4	391	4.89	P<.01
	4 - 4½	356		

Where interactions with other children were concerned, Youngest children interacted significantly more with their siblings than Eldest children. There were no differences according to the independent variables in the time spent in social interaction with children other than siblings. To see if the boys spent more time with other boys and the girls with their own sex, we compared the amount of social interaction according to sex of non-sibling children and this did not vary (see Table 5.12). Children were interacting as much with the opposite sex as with their own sex.

Table 5.12   Mean number of intervals spent in social interaction with siblings

Participating Individual	Family Position	Mean No. of Intervals	F Ratio	Level of Significance
	Eldest	70		
Siblings			13.86	P<.001
	Youngest	111		

Television watching, listening to the radio and records and fantasy play are included in Table 5.1 for comparative purposes, but are discussed more fully in separate chapters.

Section 2   The toys and equipment and domestic items available to the children

Toys and equipment commercially designed for children's play activities will be dealt with separately from the domestic items used by the children. Table 5.13 lists the types of commercial toys the children had available to them and is presented in rank order of the percentage of children using a particular type of toy. Categorisation and scoring procedures are given fully in Appendix 2.

A   Toys related to physical activities

Over 75 per cent of the children had the use of a toy vehicle or tricycle. Pedal cars, tricycles, bicycles with stablilisers and, with the younger children, glide-along vehicles predominated. We included in this category moon-hoppers and a few other items which involved 'bodily propulsion' but which occurred very rarely, such as sledges, pogo sticks and stilts. Boys tended to have this type of toy more than girls, but the difference is just short of significance. 'Climbables', i.e. climbing frames, slides, swings and seesaws were much rarer. They demand considerable outdoor space and are generally a semi-permanent erection. A few children used the type of large play equipment encountered in public parks and recreation grounds. Neither of these two latter categories varied across groups.

Table 5.13   Toys ranked in order of percentage of children who used them in the course of observation

Type of Object	% of Children
Mobile, rideable toys	90
Pencils, crayons etc.	79
Model transport	78
Children's balls	76
Books	73
Painting materials	73
Domestic replica toys	67
Soft toys	65
Noise-making toys	59
Blackboards, colouring books	57
Replicas of adult leisure activities	56
Free construction toys	53
Arrange and Shape toys	52
Girl dolls	49
Pictures and wrappers	47
Weapons	46
Miniature skilled physical toys	45
Sand Play items	41
Commercial dressing up items	40
Small model people	38
Commercial water play and swimming items	37
Toy bats, racquets and clubs	32
Accessories to model buildings	31
Large model animals	30
Non-durable home-made toys	26
Commercial toy boxes	26
Climbable toys	25
Small model animals	23
Comics and pamphlets	22
Model buildings	22

Table 5.13   (2) con'd

Type of Object	% of Children
Personality dolls	22
Specific construction toys	21
All-age intellectual hobbies and games	20
Commercial collage items	20
Unidentifiable toy remains	17
Boy dolls	16
Letter equipment	16
All-age balls, e.g. footballs, cricket balls	15
Automatic musical toys	14
Number equipment	12
All-age bats, e.g. cricket, tennis racquets	10
Children's records	8
Letter and number equipment	8
String and threading materials	7
Walk-in models	6
Public large play equipment	5

Bats and rackets were relatively rare but the majority of children had balls. Balls ranged from tiny power balls to large beach balls and many children owned a wide variety. We did distinguish between 'adult' and 'toy' balls, 'adult' balls being proper leather footballs or rugger balls and cricket balls, but the incidence of 'adult' games balls was low. We therefore combined both category of ball and boys tended to own more balls than girls.

There was no variation with the independent variables in the incidence of the group items we categorised as 'Miniature physical items'. These all required minimal physical effort from the child and some manipulative skill, and ranged from collections of marbles to yo-yos.

B   Toys related to play with materials

Approximately 40 per cent of the children had commercially designed sand or water toys. Sand toys were spades and buckets, sieves and rakes, while water play items were the type of floating things usually designed for the bath. We also included inflatable toys and swimming aids and paddling pools in this category. Equivalent numbers of sand and water toys were found among all groups.

Only 15 per cent of the children had any type of commercial soft modelling material or equipment. The materials were plasticine, Play Doh, commercial clay and Das. One or two children had the Play Doh factory and toy potter's wheel and a number had modelling moulds of animal or abstract design. Similarly, the incidence of 'fold, cut and glue' items was sporadic. We included here commercial scrap books, various cut out sets, children's scissors, and glue and glitter for sticking on to paper. Commercially produced string and weaving sets were rare; 7 per cent of the children had lacing or sewing cards or weaving sets.

Drawing implements, such as pencils, crayons and chalks were widespread. We excluded implements definitely not intended for the child's own use, for example, a parent's Parker pen. Middle class children tended to have a wider selection of these. Commercial objects designed for children to draw on were less common; 57 per cent of the children had blackboards, colouring books or more specific objects such as a spirograph or an Etcha-sketch set. We categorised together all painting equipment, from books to the paint itself and 73 per cent of the children had some type of painting equipment, although, again, the middle class children tended to be better supplied than the working class children.

We distinguished between two types of construction toys: 'Free Construction Sets' where the child was relatively unrestrained as to how he put the items together and 'Specifically Determined Construction Sets' where the pieces fitted to form a definite end product. Examples of the former are Lego, blocks and Sticklebricks and of the latter, nesting dolls and stacking cups. Middle class children were more likely to have 'Free Construction' items than the working class children. Sixty-four per cent of the middle class children had, (and used) these toys, compared with 44 per cent of the working class children ($\chi^2 = 5.5$; d.f. 1; $P<0.02$). The pattern is very similar with items which we classified as 'Arrange and Shape toys' such as jigsaw puzzles, floor puzzles and posting boxes and balls. Sixty-five per cent of the middle class children played with them, 40 per cent of the working class group ($\chi^2 = 9.5$; d.f. 1; P<0.01).

Simple noise-making instruments were much commoner than the more elaborate automatic musical toys. Whistles, drums and party squeakers were counted as simple 'noise' toys, while automatic musical toys took the form of musical boxes, record playing musical trains, toy record players and radios and televisions which emitted sounds. The numbers of, and type of, noise toy did not vary between the different sub-groups of the sample.

C   Reading, letter and number materials

We included in the book category children's puzzle books which often contained a few pages for colouring, arguing that they were very similar to the hard back collections of pictures and puzzles. Ladybird and Mister Men books were popular, the middle class children having access to significantly more books than the working class children (see Table 5.14). We categorised comics and pamphlets together: young children's comics such as Beano, Trixie and Twinkle and pamphlets designed for young children, such as Lego and Airfix leaflets and the Green Cross Code pamphlet. While 73 per cent of the children had at least one book, under half the children had pamphlets and there was no significant class difference with the latter. We also thought that cards, pictures and wrappers designed for children often provide important pre-reading material and so these were quantified. Cards included greeting cards and also 'collectable' cards of football stars and vintage cars. The incidence of these items did not vary with any of the independent variables.

Table 5.14   Books

	Class	Mean No. of Items per Child	F Ratio	Level of Significance
Books	M	7		
			15.56	P<0.001
	W	3		

The incidence of commercially designed letter and number equipment was low. Number equipment consisted of educational clocks of various types, abaci, and, also included here, blocks with moulded numbers. The Fisher-Price Play Desk was the only combined letter and number item encountered. Letter equipment included plastic alphabet sets and charts and lined school-type excercise books. Although numbers are low, middle class children were significantly more likely to have some form of letter equipment. Twenty-four per cent of them did, while only 9 per cent of the working class children used them ($\chi^2 = 5.9$; d.f. 1; P<0.01).

D Dolls, model people and animals

Dolls now come in a variety of shapes, sizes and personae. We were interested to see whether the relatively recent development of boy dolls such as 'Action Man' would have led to an increased ownership of dolls by boys. In order not to obscure this possibility we had three separate 'doll' categories. All female dolls from large baby dolls and tiny baby dolls to teenage female dolls and figures such as a Bionic Woman were classified as 'Girl dolls'. These dolls varied considerably in complexity; some were merely plastic shapes with immoveable limbs, while an exceptional doll could be fed with special food, chew, and dirty and wet its nappy. Eighty-four per cent of the girls had 'Girl dolls' and played with them in the course of observation, while only 17 per cent of the boys did so ($\chi^2 = 72$; d.f. 1; P<0.001). The second category was 'Boy dolls'. The incidence of these was low; 16 per cent of the children had one and boys were not more likely to have them than girls. The third category, 'Personality dolls', consisted of dolls which were not clearly of either sex, and, again, with these dolls there was no difference in ownership. All dolls, regardless of sex and whether human or animal representations, if made of soft fabric, were classified as 'Soft toys', as we considered the feel of the object was its most potent characteristic. Therefore, rag dolls, teddy bears, cuddly and furry animals of all types are included here and again there is a significant sex difference, with girls playing with soft toys more than boys, i.e. 79 per cent of the girls and 52 per cent of the boys ($\chi^2 = 12.00$; d.f. 2; P<0.001).

We separated large model farm animals from smaller models as children frequently had large collections of farm or zoo animals, whereas large models appeared as unique items. Only 23 per cent of the children had collections of small model animals but where they did occur they were in large collections.

The same was true for small model people, such as soldiers, cowboys and Indians and Weebles. About a third of the sample, 38 per cent, had this type of toy and again when children did have them, they had large collections. The incidence of both small model animals and small model people did not vary with any of the independent variables. A similar number of children had large model animals such as 'Jaws', a large plastic shark, or a large toy cow, crocodile or horse. Here the incidence increased significantly with age; from 16 per cent of the 3–3½-year-olds, 33 per cent of the 3½–4-year-olds to 44 per cent of the 4–4½-year-olds ($\chi^2 = 9.9$; d.f. 2; $P < 0.01$).

E Toy replicas of items in adult life

These items, like small model people and animals, are all designed to be played with in a fantasy manner, particularly for what we have defined as representational fantasy play (see Chapter 7). The toys have few other potential activity stimulating qualities. We postulated that it would be among this type of toy that sex differences might be particularly apparent and so the toy categorisation is designed to separate these toys according to conventional sex role expectations. All domestic toy equipment was placed in one category. Examples ranged widely: plastic replicas of fruit, vegetables and breakfast cereal packets; toy cutlery, kitchen equipment and tea services; doll's bedding and furniture; toy hair clips, cookers and ironing boards. The girls did have and use far more of these types of items than the boys. The reverse was true for what we labelled 'Model transport', which included toy cars, lorries, buses, aeroplanes, trains, etc. Here the boys had significantly more than the girls (see Table 5.15).

We included all guns, swords and bows and arrows under the heading of weapons. Only 46 per cent of the children took part in activities with toy weapons and significantly more boys (59 per cent) than girls (31 per cent) used weapons ($\chi^2 = 11.6$; d.f. 2; $P < 0.001$).

Commercial dressing up items were entered in one category and split according to conventional sex role criteria. Forty per cent of

Table 5.15   Domestic and model transport toys

Toy	Sex	Mean Items per Child	F Ratio	Level of Significance
Domestic	m	1	80.75	P<0.001
	f	7		
Model Transport	m	16	100.76	P<0.001
	f	3		

the children had at least one item in this category. Cowboy outfits, police and nurses' uniforms were included along with items such as toy sunglasses and watches. The incidence of commercial dressing up items was inclined to increase with age.

A very small number of children had Wendy Houses or tents which were large enough for the child to enter himself. Smaller models of buildings were more common but still quite rare, only 22 per cent of the children having this type of toy. These included garages, dolls' houses, stations, forts, the 'Live and Learn Play Book' and the Fisher-Price 'Model Tree House', and were evenly spread across all groups of children.

In the category 'Accessories to Model Buildings' boys (41 per cent) had significantly more than girls (20 per cent), ($x^2 = 7.7$; d.f. 1; P<0.01). We had included toys like dolls' house furniture in the 'Domestic replica' category, and so this category included items such as railway tracks, farm fences, lamp posts, petrol pumps, bridges and tiny ladders.

Toy replicas of adult occupational and leisure activities were again not divided according to conventional sex roles. Many of the items were indeed 'unisex'. These items varied from specific 'occupational' sets such as a medical case containing pill boxes, a stethoscope and hypodermic syringe, to toy garden tools and items like toy binoculars and cameras. Their incidence did not vary between groups.

F Miscellaneous categories

Eight per cent of the children had records specifically made for children, such as Nursery Rhyme records or, for instance, a Womble record. Pop records which were more common were not included in this category. We quantified children's commercially designed toy boxes and included here manufacturers' containers which were designed to be durable such as Lego sacks. Inevitably some toy remains were unidentifiable and these were grouped into one category. None of these three categories varied significantly across the different groups.

All-age table games and hobbies consisted of items such as Ludo, Scrabble and stamp collecting, which are generally participated in by children, particularly older children, but also by adults. There was a tendency for Youngest children to have contact with more of these items than the other two groups, the Eldest children having the least contact. A variety of items were recorded which the child made for himself or someone in the family made for him which were toys with only fleeting life expectancies. There were things such as paper aeroplanes, egg box monsters, matchbox cars, and strings of newspaper dolls. Their incidence increased significantly with the age of the subjects. Only 15 per cent of the youngest age group had this type of home-made toy, rising to 27 per cent among the 3½–4-year-olds and 40 per cent in the 4–4½-year-olds (χ^2 = 8.61; d.f. 2; $P<0.01$).

G Range of toys

The system of categorisation was designed specifically to overcome the problem of the heterogeneity of the toys. However, we wished to perform some type of overall comparison of the children's toys and therefore computed a variable to indicate the range of toys the individual children possessed. Each separate category was scored as absent or present, i.e. ignoring the number of toys in the category and then a total score computed of the number of categories represented. Across the entire sample the mean number of categories was 16.5. There was no significant social class difference, but the scores in the working class group showed much greater variation than those of the middle class group.

Domestic Items and Equipment Available to Children

The percentage of children who used different types of domestic items is presented in Table 5.16.

Table 5.16   Domestic items ranked in order of percentage of children who used them in the course of observation

Type of Object	% of Children
Indoor furniture	99
Electric entertainment devices	93
Cookery implements and crockery	88
Clothing	88
Edible household consumables	86
Empty commercial containers	79
Natural objects	77
Non-powered cleaning implements	75
Soft furnishings	74
Tools	68
Jewellry and accessories	65
Family paper	62
Adult non-leisure reading materials	58
Outside items, e.g. dustcarts, aeroplanes	58
Durable toiletries, e.g. hair brushes, rollers	56
Ornaments and pictures	56
Outdoor furniture	52
Observer's possessions	50
Inedible household consumables	49
Cosmetics, toiletries and medicines	49
Powered domestic appliances	47
Domestic spares, e.g. fuse wire, batteries	46
Sewing/knitting items	44
Children's functional equipment	42

Domestic family pets	42
Adult leisure reading	41
Wild animals, e.g. earthworms, sparrows	38
Areas and rooms	35
Domestic pets, other than family's	30
Money	29
Hardware rubbish items	21
Animal equipment	18
Children's furniture	18
Unidentified domestic objects	10
Items connected with adult occupations	10
Adult records and tapes	10
Adult musical instrument	4

H Domestic supplies and kitchen equipment

Nearly all the children in the sample used 'Cookery implements and crockery' in their activities during observation. The same was true for 'Edible' but not for 'Inedible household consumables'. 'Edible consumables' ranged from salt to beer, Rice Krispies or pre-pared vegetables. 'Inedible consumables' were predominantly cleaning materials, such as Windowlene and bleach, but also included oddments such as elastic bands and drawing pins, and only 49 per cent of the children were involved with this item. Seventy-five per cent of the children used non-powered cleaning imple-ments, such as brushes or mops. None of these items varied bet-ween the different sample groups. Nearly 80 per cent of the children used empty commercial containers in their activities, such as mar-garine tubs, squeezy detergent bottles, or cardboard boxes and these tended to be available more in the middle class homes, but this just does not approach significance at the 0.01 level. We included under one heading all domestic paper such as lavatory paper, bags, grease-proof paper and incidental bits of paper acquired in domes-tic routine, i.e. till receipts, bus tickets and price tickets. Again the incidence did not vary across groups.

I Cosmetics and toiletries

'Cosmetics, toiletries and medical products' included all types of creams and powders, from baby lotion, face cream to Vick ointment and other medical and cosmetic items. Girls tended to use these items more in their activities than boys. In contrast, 'Durable toiletries' were non-disposable items connected also with personal care, such as eyebrow tweezers, shaving brushes and hair rollers. Sixty-five per cent of the girls used these items compared with 57 per cent of the boys. The difference is significant ($\chi^2 = 6.8$; d.f. 2; P<0.01).

J Clothing, jewellery and accessories

All items of clothing used in the child's play activities were placed in this category, regardless of ownership. A high proportion, 80 per cent of the children, used clothing in their play at some time. Girls used significantly more items in this way than boys (mean number of items: m 3, f6; F = 20.5; P<0.001). More girls, 62 per cent as opposed to 45 per cent of the boys ($\chi^{2} = 9.9$; d.f. 1; P<0.002) played with 'Jewellery and personal accessories.'

K Items for domestic maintenance

Only 44 per cent of the children had contact with items concerned with sewing and knitting and the incidence showed no variation across groups. A number of households kept a supply of what we termed 'Domestic spares', such as fuse wire, spare batteries and light bulbs. We distinguished 'Domestic spares' from 'Hardware rubbish' items in that the former were in a new or re-usable condition. Boys tended to use the Rubbish items more than girls and significantly more of the 'Domestic spares' than the girls. Similarly, boys were attracted to 'Tools' more than were girls, these being tools used for maintenance, electrical repair, gardening, carpentry and house decoration (see Table 5.17).

Table 5.17   Percentage of children who used 'Domestic spares' and 'Tools'

Item	Sex	Used Item	Did Not Use Item	2	Level of Significance
Domestic	m	55	45		
				8.73	P<0.005
Spares	f	31	69		
	m	71	29		
Tools				19.78	P<0.001
	f	44	56		

L Furniture and furnishings

Almost all the children incorporated indoor furniture into their activities at some time. We distinguished indoor from outdoor furniture, which fewer children had access to. Children's furniture, such as children's desks and chairs, was categorised separately and was distinct from 'Children's functional equipment' such as baby-walkers or bouncers, playpens and trainer lavatory seats. Adult 'ornaments and pictures' and 'Soft furnishings' such as cushions, bedding and carpets were two further separate categories. None of these items varied with any of the independent variables.

M Animals and animal equipment

We wished to see how many of the children had domestic pets at home and so we separated these from domestic pets which belonged to people outside the family, such as next door neighbours and relations. Forty-two per cent of the children had contact with family pets, which were most commonly dogs, cats, goldfish and tropical fish and budgerigars. Thirty per cent of the children encountered other people's domestic pets. Wild animals we coded separately and these consisted mainly of ladybirds, earthworms and wild birds. All animal equipment was coded in one category, such as birdcages, dog leads and flea powder. None of these animals or animal equipment categories varied significantly with any of the independent variables.

N Items connected with adult leisure and occupational activities

We divided adult reading material into 'Leisure' and 'Non-leisure' groupings, i.e. novels, newspapers and magazines as opposed to official documents, telephone directories and mail order catalogues. Neither varied with the independent variables. Few children encountered adult records and tapes and it tended to occur more with boys than with girls. Only 4 per cent of the children had contact with adult musical instruments during the course of observation. Items connected with parental occupations ranged from a bus conductor's ticket machine, a mother's typewriter, to a salesman's order forms. Ninteen per cent of the middle class children had these objects available to them compared with 3 per cent of the working class ($\chi^2 = 8.8$; d.f. 1; P<0.01).

O Electric entertainment devices and powered domestic appliances

'Electric entertainment devices' were items such as televisions, radios, record players, tape recorders and projectors. There was a tendency for the incidence to increase with the children's age. This was not true for the large category of 'Powered domestic appliances' which did not vary with any of the independent variables.

P 'Outside items' and 'natural objects'

'Outside items' were items which the child encountered in public or commercial places and were things such as telephone kiosks, a fishmonger's window display or a helicopter flying past. Boys showed significantly more interest in these types of things (see Table 5.18). This was not true of 'Natural objects', which were growing plants and such things as the sun, icicles and earth.

Table 5.18 'Outside items'

	Sex	Mean No. of Items per Child	F Ratio	Level of Significance
'Outside' Items	m	3		
			7.30	P<0.01
	f	1		

Q Miscellaneous domestic item categories

Twenty nine per cent of the children had contact with real money, either notes or coins. Frequently children kept a few small coins in an old purse or money box, or occasionally, on shopping expeditions, a child would be given the correct coin to pay for some sweets for himself. 'Areas and rooms' were usually small, enclosed spaces such as pantries, stairs, garden sheds. Inevitably, there were a certain number of unidentifiable domestic objects, not rubbish, which were placed in a separate category. We considered that interest in the observer's possessions might show a consistent variation according to one of the independent variables, but this was not so, and none of the categories in the last paragraph varied significantly with any of the independent variables.

Discussion and conclusions

The range of activities is wide, and as a result the time spent in any one single activity is short. The children were well provided with toys and while three children from the working class group did stand out as having fewer toys compared with all the other children, even they would have fulfilled Pollak's criterion of having three age appropriate toys in the home (Pollak, 1972). This compares with Pollak's findings, in the Lambeth sample, of 7 per cent of the English and 80 per cent of the West Indian children not meeting this criterion. Our children used a great many domestic items in their activities. With regard to these items, preferences showed most variation with the sex of the child.

The little girls chose to use traditionally female objects in their activities, such as 'Jewellery' and 'Personal accessories', 'Durable toiletries' and clothing, while the boys preferred tools, 'Domestic spares' and 'Hardware rubbish' items. These sexual preferences were mirrored in the toy items with which the children played; the girls with their dolls, soft toys and domestic replica toys, and the boys with their weapons, toy cars, trucks, trains, railway tracks and petrol pumps. Behaviourally, the boys spent more time in building and constructing things, for which they used both conventional toys and also the bits and bobs included in 'Hardware rubbish'. Girls spent longer packing small items into containers, these often being old handbags and purses. The girls' fondness for clothing is repeated in the extra time which they spent in dressing up. While an attempt at a definitive 'nature-nurture' discussion would be fruitless, it was noticeable in incidental observations of family life that no mothers were seen to mend cars, use carpentry or heavy gardening tools and very few fathers did any type of housework. However, explicit references to encourage the child to conform to a particular sex role were few and far between. One working class mother, for instance, restrained her son from dragging his little girl friend off the settee by the neck, saying, 'Little girls don't like rough play' and a middle class father, who spent a great deal of time with his children, explained his feelings and motives to the observer after an observation session:

'I'm really saving myself for John' (infant brother of two older sisters). 'He's the important one. I'm afraid I'm old-fashioned and still agree with this idea. He's definitely the most important and I'll be starting work on him soon. After all, girls can just please themselves; they don't need a career like men do, they're the bread winners'. (Quotation from notes made immediately after the session ended).

These cases were exceptional.

Conventional sexually stereotyped behaviour occurred less obviously with the boys' preference for throwing, kicking, hitting and waving objects, from balls to sticks, stones and tiddley-winks. This was not attributable to a male preference for physical activity because the girls spent more time running, jumping and climbing, although this did not approach statistical significance. In their extensive review of sex differences, Maccoby and Jacklin (1975) conclude that there is a male superiority in spatial ability, but this advantage is not apparent until children are approximately eight years old. Ball play and skilled miniature physical play could certainly be tapping or feeding this advantage. Another point is that kicking a ball is a far simpler task than catching or hitting one with a bat or racquet and therefore may be more rewarding for children of this age. Also, despite the recent growth in the number of female football teams, football is still viewed as predominantly a male sport. While the precise type of ball play was not recorded, the majority of boys went in for football type play and almost none of the girls did so. The fact that this is the one activity in which more fathers participated with their sons than with their daughters reinforces this point.

There is evidence that 'Gross physical play', often labelled rough and tumble play, is engaged in more by boys than girls. For example, Whiting and Edwards (1973) reported this to be the case in a wide variety of cultural settings, with children aged between 3-11 years; Langlois, Gottfried and Seay (1973) and Di Pietro (1981) among Nursery School children. This has led to theoretical speculation on the role of 'Gross physical play' in the development of aggressive skills (Hartup, 1974). If boys stimulate this type of play (Halverson and Waldrop, 1973), it could well be that the sex difference is enhanced in a group setting, such as a Nursery School, where children have a choice in the sex of their playmates compared to the fortuitous and relatively restricted range of play partners available to the child at home. While fathers, in this study, were available to their children for much less of the day than mothers and interacted much less with their children, nearly as many fathers did take part in this type of play as the mothers.

Vehicle riding was an activity in which boys predominated. Tizard, Philps and Plewis (1976) report a marked social class difference in preschool centres in terms of vehicle play, the working class children spending twice as much time outside on wheeled vehicles as the middle class children. A social class difference was not evident in this study where the children were home based, neither in availability of wheeled toys nor in time spent using them. The study of Tizard *et al.*, (ibid.) was London based and therefore the working class children may not have had the space for wheeled vehicle play at home, unlike the working class Stoke sample. Another possibility is, as the authors suggest, that the working class children were using outdoor vehicle play to avoid nursery staff contact, and therefore no difference in the children's behaviour at home should be expected. In our study, boys appeared both to particularly enjoy the sensation of pedalling about, sometimes over bumps constructed by them from planks and tins and incorporating vehicle riding into their fantasy play when they became policemen, firemen, ambulance drivers, etc.

While there was no social class difference in the overall number of toys, the middle class children were better provided with a few specific types of item. Although the type of simple and specific construction toys did not vary, possibly because these toys are more appropriate for younger children and we were only seeing the remnants of toys from when the children were younger, the middle class children did have access to more 'Free' construction toys and more jig-saw puzzle-type toys. Parents were not asked about their toy buying tactics, whether they or the child chose his toys, or what their rationale was for buying them. One possible reason for this social class difference could be expense. Packets of Lego or wooden jig-saws are very expensive relative to their spectacular appeal and whereas the working class parents might have been able and prepared to spend a very large sum of money on an item such as a new bicycle or a very glamorous doll, the prices of these other items might have appeared relatively too high. Both jig-saws and construction toys have an 'aura' of educational respectability about them which might have attracted the middle class parents. They involve fitting and matching shapes and colours and jig-saws offer a clear and satisfactory end product as a reward for concentration and 'Free Construction' toys in addition give rein to the child's imagination.

Middle class children did spend more time than the working class children in 'Arrange and shape' activities, not only with conventional toys but with a variety of objects. Unlike replica toys, both 'Free Construction' and jig-saw type toys need to be introduced to children, who must be shown initially what can be done with them. While there is no significant difference for class in the number of adults who engaged in 'Arrange and shape' activities with their children, more middle class adults did this. Because so few children had adult time spent on them in this way, it was impossible to test this statistically, but more middle class adult time was spent with the children in 'Arrange and shape' activities. Both measures suggest that it may be the adult participation which encourages the middle class children compared with working class children to engage in more 'Arrange and shape' activities. Possibly, as middle class parents are prepared to put in this extra time, this influences their own toy buying decisions.

The method we used for toy quantification probably underestimated the number of books which were available to children. In contrast to toys, children were unlikely to pull out every book they owned in the course of observation, if there were several shelves full. Therefore, while the pattern of book ownership and the preponderance among the middle class children is valid, the differences between the social classes may be wider. Few middle class children were without their own books, usually kept in special shelves in their bedrooms or in the sitting room. This was also true for a number of the working class children, but quite a few of these children only owned the odd book which lived with their other toys or lay about the sitting room. Although the difference does not in any way near significance, the working class children did have more comics than the middle class children and often these were referred to by the family as 'books', as were adult magazines.

This lack of distinction between children's books, usually containing a story, and more general printed material was reflected in the use the parents made of printed material, in that there was no clear difference in terms of 'Looking at books' but a clear difference when the children were 'Read to'. Listening to someone else reading is an activity which requires experience, even if the child is looking at the acompanying pictures with the adult. The ability to sit and listen requires more maturity on the part of the child. This difference is also likely to be reflecting cultural differences on the part of the parents. If the middle class parents did in fact read more than the working class parents, it would be a natural step for them to read out loud to their children. One measure we regretted not taking was a simple estimate of whether shelves of adult books were present in the home. Our incidental impression was that this was class-related and that few of the working class homes had the large collections of books found in some, but by no means all, of the middle class homes.

We had anticipated that more of the middle class children would be provided with specific letter and number equipment and that their parents would perhaps be taking definite steps to teach their children to count and read. In fact, only two children were actually observed in flash card sessions with their mothers. From parents' comments it seemed that teaching a child to write his name was a separate and admirable activity, whereas teaching him to read was dangerous in that it stepped into the preserves of the teacher and mis-teaching would be harmful to the child when he eventually went to school. One working class mother who participated very little in any activities with her son, explained to the observer that she deliberately avoided 'doing' anything with the child in case she did it wrong and it was better to leave it to the teachers when he got to school. This woman was a very competent housewife and from her behaviour with her other domestic affairs it did seem to be a deliberate policy and not a reflection of lethargy or inadequacy.

While a high proportion of children drew and crayoned, painting was more often encountered with the middle class children; contrary to drawing or crayoning, painting needs considerable preparation. Water pots have to be filled and furniture protected from potential mess and this needs adult initiative and some participation, which may account for the difference.

The incidence of other forms of 'messy' play were low across the entire sample. Few children experienced soft modelling and similarly collage work was brief and rarely done. That the middle class children had more empty tubs, boxes and cartons to play with may reflect Play Group influences. While programmes such as 'Blue Peter' or 'Magpie' on television were seen and suggest exciting uses for these types of objects, they are geared to slightly older children. Play Groups make very full use of 'junk' materials and most mothers of Play Group attenders are besieged with demands for egg boxes and squeezy bottles. Play Group attendance was significantly higher among the middle class children (see Chapter 9) and the Play Group ethos is likely to spill over from the Group to the home.

Another group of activities which were remarkable for their infrequency were domestic activities. Cooking is a unique means of providing a child with a variety of stimulating experiences. There seem to have been two contributory factors to this lack of participation. Cooking in most families consisted of frying, grilling and warming convenience foods, all of which involve minimal preparation time and therefore lack potential for child involvement. Baking is the type of cooking which provides most opportunity for the child to take part and few mothers made their own cakes, pastries or bread. However, even if the preparation time is brief, there are still opportunities for the child, for instance, to tip the contents of the tin into the saucepan, or whip the 'blancmange' powder into the milk. As this rarely occurred, parents were also *choosing* not to involve the child. Children spent very little time in other types of domestic activity; while a few participated, most played at their own activities while their mothers did their daily chores and got on with their jobs. Where a child actually assisted his father with the gardening, or stripping off wallpaper, the case stood out as exceptional. Children were more likely to watch the parent at work and then move on to their own activities.

It is much easier and quicker to do a job without the harassment of small children joining in, but as most parents were prepared to spend time on 'play' activities with children, the time element does not seem to be crucial. One possibility is that before the Second World War, when birth control was not so wide-spread and working class standards of living were much lower, a child in a large working class family would have had to have helped his parents in numerous ways in order for the family to have survived domestically. It is a sign of affluence when children's help is not essential in the home and when older children can spend the evenings doing their homework rather than housework. To parents with memories of working class childhoods or who have been brought up as the first generation of children in a family who did not have to work in the house, it may be important that children do not have to participate in domestic chores and the idea that participation is itself enjoyable and beneficial to children may be alien.

Age differences, both in terms of behaviour and toy provision, were slight. Home-made toys were found more as the children grew older and became more competent in making toys and objects themselves, albeit very simple objects. Children also became less prone to spend time exploring objects visually and tactilely, which would be expected as this behaviour peaks in late infancy. Similarly, unspecific rolling about on the floor declined steadily with age. Searching for specific objects linked to a future activity increased with age, reflecting the child's growing capacity to plan ahead for his future activities. Children were also becoming increasingly independent, as shown by the decreasing amount of child-adult interaction with age.

Time spent in social interactions with other people also varied with the child's position in the family. Youngest children received least

adult time and in particular were given comparatively little attention by their fathers. We had expected the sex of the child to affect
the amount of parental interaction, but this was not evident with
either mothers or fathers. It may be that sex is a potent variable but
is related in such a complex way to the sex of other siblings in the
family and our sample was not large enough to examine this aspect
of the variable.

There are several possible reasons for apparent paternal neglect
of their Youngest children. The father will have already established
a tradition of interaction with the older siblings before the Youngest
child is on the scene. The Youngest child was competing with a sibling usually two years older, therefore more socially mature and
adroit and better equipped to win adult attention. The birth of a
younger child may well increase the relationship between the first
born child and the father as the new baby requires the type of care
typically given by the mother; the father may then compensate by
giving more attention to the older child, which would explain why
family position did not affect maternal interaction but did have a
strong effect on paternal interaction.

While the Youngest children received less adult interaction, they
engaged most in activities with other children, the participants
being predominantly their older siblings. While Eldest, Only and
Youngest children interacted an equivalent amount with children
outside the family, we had anticipated that Only children might
have an increased amount of interaction here, but this was not the
case.

There is a large difference in the amount of sibling interaction
between the Eldest and Youngest children. Few Eldest children had
more than one sibling, a few came from three children families and
one exceptional child was the Eldest of four. Generally, the younger
siblings were babies or toddlers. The Eldest child was in a position
to control any social interation with his younger sibling. If the sibling was a young baby it was up to the older child to initiate any
interaction, which was limited by the immaturity of the young child.
Even if the younger child was mobile or more advanced, the elder
was still the dominant partner and could withdraw when expedient. Eldest children did spend significantly more time in 'Miniature social play' compared with Youngest children, in behaviour
appropriate to the needs of a baby or toddler. In contrast, the
Youngest children in our sample, though older and more socially

competent then the very young siblings of the Eldest children, were still the subordinate partners in social exchanges, yet were old enough to pursue elder siblings in order to join in their activities. Frequently, Youngest children tagged on to their older brothers and sisters and their friends. Often it was the friends who prevented the younger child from being excluded. Youngest children took part in more game playing than the older two groups. This was an activity which required a child older than our sample age to initiate and organise and therefore was likely to occur only when an older child was about. Youngest children also had more table games available to them, again provided from the older siblings' toys.

Only children took part least in physical activities such as running, jumping and climbing, as they lacked the stimulation provided by siblings for this type of activity. Mothers of Only children compensated for their children's lack of siblings by taking part in activities which parents of more than one child presumably had no need to do, such as vehicle riding and pushing children on swings and trolleys. Only children also spent least time 'Watching other people'. We would suggest that this is because they had both less children to watch, i.e. in the absence of siblings, but also because instead of watching their parents they were more inclined to actively participate in what the adult was doing, which would correspond with the greater assertivenes of Only children compared to Eldest and Youngest children, found by Snow, Jacklin and Maccoby (1981).

The pattern of activities and toy preferences accords in many respects with that reported to the Newsons by the parents of seven-year-olds in Nottingham (1976). Drawing was the children's most frequently mentioned activity; middle class children read and wrote for pleasure more than the working class children but they also found that both these activities were preferred by girls. Bicycling was popular with all children, as was ball play, but with the latter the girls liked bouncing balls and the boys football. Middle class children were reported to have more jig-saw puzzles than working class children, and constructive toys were played with more by boys than girls, with middle class boys having more Lego. The sex differences between domestic toys and toy cars we have found also hold in the Newsons' data.

Thus the differences in the children's facilities and toys attributable to social class are not outstanding but, whereas the provision of toys among the middle class group was very even overall, the provision among the working class children showed more individual variation numerically and qualitatively. Age differences were also few. Our measures may not have picked up subtle qualitative differences in activities which would have embraced both social class and age differences, but the child with little time spent on him and with few toys was the exception, and the less time accorded by adults to Youngest children, compared with Eldest and Only children, cut across both social class and sex boundaries. Parents tended to concentrate on child-centred activities when participating with their children and also to show reticence in teaching their children things which they considered were the province of the professional in the school.

Chapter 6
Fantasy play

The imaginative or fantasy play of children is an outstanding and entertaining aspect of 'childishness'. Classical writers on education have commented on this attribute but opinions have varied as to whether 'pretend' play should be deliberately encouraged or prevented. Froebel (trans. 1912) considered that the child's limited experience of the real world could be verbally extended by, for instance, a deliberate exercise in 'the First Play': 'The dangling ball now becomes many things, as a bird, as a kitten, a dog .. so that from this one object the child in his imagination forms many.' Dewey (1900) disagreed with this aspect of Froebel's writing and argued that objects must be known before they could be used. Montessori considered that it was pernicious to attempt to cultivate childish imaginings as she maintained they represented an immature state of development and therefore children should be educated to overcome them. She argued that rich children who rode real ponies did not need to whip a stick and create an illusion ... 'this is not proof of an imagination, it is proof of an unsatisfied desire'.

Margaret McMillan, on the contrary, who had a profound influence on the early British preschool educational movement, is often cited as an originator of support and encouragement of imaginative play in the classroom. In her book, 'Education through the Imagination' (1904), she used the term 'imagination' in a way which makes its precise definition impossible and included such attributes as power of abstraction, freedom of physical movement and memory development. In her Preface, she stated:

The child mind develops then mainly through the free activity of imagination. To suppress or ignore this faculty at that period means the suppression of all the faculties – latent as well as developed. Freedom of invention and creation in its freest form – in play, tales, etc must be secured at the sacrifice, if necessary, of all formal arts and training.

Similarly, Susan Isaacs (1930; 1933) was an advocate of the need for children's imaginitive or fantasy to be encouraged in the classroom. She saw it as a means of dealing with the children's emotions.

Much more recently, Sara Smilansky (1968) produced her influential book on socio-dramatic play in preschool children. She defined socio-dramatic play as play where the child pretended to be someone else, and elaborated the theme with the co-operation of another participant. She assessed the quality of the play in terms of a six point rating scale. Using descriptive reports of play in Israeli Nursery Schools, she concluded that there were profound differences in the quality and quantity of the socio-dramatic play of advantaged and disadvantaged children. Advantaged children she described as coming from predominantly middle and high social economic backgrounds, while disadvantaged children came from Middle Eastern immigrant parents. In the one aspect of the study which she quantified (the themes selected by the children), she found no differences between the two types of children. However, she considered there were basic differences in areas in which she had not quantified: advantaged children showed more elaboration and flexibility in developing a theme; advantaged children used props which were less well defined as play objects; leadership was exercised differently between the two types of children, advantaged children organising themselves democratically and disadvantaged children autocratically; disadvantaged children played roles in a stereotyped manner, lacking the rational understanding and the consequent flexibility of advantaged children's role playing. Smilansky considered that the differences she describes were attributable to the divergent cultures the two groups of children experienced at home. She also reported age differences in enactment of socio-dramatic play, but considered that although disadvantaged children progressed to some extent to attain play levels advantaged children had reached earlier, the performance remained qualitatively different. Smilansky considered intelligence was not a main variable affecting socio-dramatic play, because both advantaged and disadvantaged children were widely distributed in their measured intelligence quotients.

Arguing that dramatic play was a means of furthering the intellectual and social development of the preschool child, Smilansky then 'trained' experimentally three groups of disadvantaged children. She reported that the group who received training both in knowledge and understanding and in techniques of play showed an improvement in the quality of their play. She therefore concluded that the training was highly beneficial to the children. Smilansky considered statistics inappropriate to her form of analysis and so her conclusions are based on little quantification.

Other evidence of social class differences in fantasy play has been provided by Tizard, Philps and Plewis (1976) and Smith and Dodsworth (1978) in English preschool settings and Rosen (1974) and Griffing (1980) comparing fantasy play between advantaged and disadvantaged youngsters in American Kindergartens. In all these studies, the lower class or disadvantaged children took part in less fantasy play then the middle class or advantaged children. Eifermann (1971) has suggested that the difference is attributable to developmental lag rather than ability, in that she found that children from low socio-economic backgrounds in first and second grades showed comparatively more collective fantasy play in free play periods outside.

Sherrod and Singer (1977) considered that fantasy play can have beneficial effects on the child's development and functioning. They have collated evidence to illustrate that disposition to fantasy play correlates positively with positive affect (Singer and Singer, 1973; Singer and Singer, 1976); complexity of verbal communication (Smilansky, 1968); ability to concentrate (Singer, 1973); amount of peer-play interaction and frequency of friendly peer interaction (Marshall and Doshi, 1965); and negatively with aggressive play (Biblow, 1973; Singer, 1973).

A number of studies have examined the effectiveness of fantasy play tutoring on specific aspects of the child's behaviour. Marshall and Hahn (1967) considered that fantasy training improved middle class children's social development. Feitelson (1972) reported that fantasy tutoring raised the level, according to the Smilansky rating system, of both imaginative play and the number and originality of child-initiated responses. Feitelson and Ross (1973) ascribed increases in creativity measured by changes on the 'Torrance

Creativity Tests' to fantasy tutoring. Fantasy play intervention is reported to raise intelligence quotients, by Saltz and Johnson (1974) and Saltz, Dixon and Johnson (1977), and problem solving ability (Rosen, 1974). Golomb and Cornelius (1977) considered that symbolic training taught children conservation. Schmukler and Naveh (1980) argue that fantasy tutoring is more potent in its effects with lower class children. In their study they report tutoring increasing co-operation and interaction with peers and positive affect with middle class children but also concentration and imaginativeness with lower class children. They considered that the middle class children had in effect already reached a ceiling level in concentration and imaginativeness and therefore showed no further increase. However, Smith and Syddall (1978) critically examined previous studies and argued that the gains specifically ascribed to fantasy play tutoring were arguably a function of increased adult contact, for which there had been inadequate control. They undertook a fantasy play tutoring study where tutor verbal contact across conditions was carefully matched and found that under these conditions the advantages to the play tutored subject were few and specific to the fantasy tutoring, namely an increase in fantasy play itself and in group activities. Similar results were obtained by Hutt *et al* (in preparation), in the sister research project to this, when, again, adult contact was carefully controlled.

Although social class differences and the benefits of fantasy play tutoring have not been clearly established it is currently accepted as an important aspect of institutional preschool involvement. Yardley (1973) writing for Nursery School teachers, considered that sensitive nurture of imagination in the preschool years was essential to the child's development and that imaginative action on the part of the child was important in leading to the child's first discoveries. Similarly, McCreesh and Maher (1976) adhered to Susan Isaacs' philosophy that one of the three ways in which children learn are 'through delight in make-believe and the expression of the world within'. In her book, 'The Modern Nursery', Marion Dowling (1976) described how imaginative play can be encouraged in the classroom, with its consequent benefits of the ability to act out an emotionally distressing experience and opportunities for practising co-operation, sharing, leading and generally enhancing desirable social behaviour. It appears to be a generally accepted practice that fantasy or imaginative play should be encouraged in the classroom.

Although class differences in fantasy play have been reported in institutions, there is very little evidence of whether this reflects the children's behaviour at home. Wootton (1974), using tape recordings of speech on a small sample of children, did report that parental involvement in an imaginative capacity with the child varied with social class. Freyberg (1973) found that children with high fantasy predispositions tended to be Only or Eldest children, to have more living space at home and to have more educated parents who were more tolerant and encouraging of make believe and fantasy; the children also tended to be closer to one parent, usually the mother. Singer (1973) deduced from Freyberg's findings that fantasy play was encouraged by parental participation and initiation and that children required privacy to take in and integrate their experiences. In the light of the findings reported in the literature, it was important to examine fantasy play in some detail in this study. We therefore wished to design behaviour categories that would measure the incidence of fantasy play, its quality and complexity and the participation by other people.

Piaget (1951) described symbolic games as following three stages. In Stage I, children project symbolic schemes on to new objects and project imitative schemes on to new objects. This develops to the child showing simple identification of one object with another; the child identifying his own body with that of other people or with things. These identifications may be in simple combinations, with the transpositions of real scenes. The scenes may compensate for what the child lacks in real life; they may emancipate the child from what has been a distressing incident in real life; at their most advanced they may anticipate and act out a potentially distressing situation. In Stage II, Piaget considered that the child, now aged four to seven years approximately, shows more reality, orderliness and exactitude in his symbolic play. Also, he shows more 'collective symbolism', sharing roles and symbols with other participating children. By Stage III, after seven or eight years of age, symbolism is declining and games with rules or symbolic construction are rising in importance in the child's play.

Our categorisation has been influenced by the Piagetian scheme. We have deliberately called this aspect of the child's behaviour 'fantasy play' to avoid the possible assumption of creativity implicit in the term imaginative play as used by Nursery School staff, while 'symbolic play' suggests a too close adherence to the Piagetian framework. Overall, fantasy play is defined as any behaviour on the part of the child which involves an element of 'let's pretend'. Fantasy play is deduced from the child's overt and vocal behaviour. Four basic categories for recording are used.

Fantasy play categories

1 REPRESENTATIONAL OBJECT

Use of representational objects, e.g. toy models of adult objects and real adult objects, in conventionally simulated situations, e.g. pushing a toy car along making motor noises or sitting in parents' car, twisting the steering wheel and making car noises.

2 FANTASY OBJECT PLAY

The object changes character in the child's imagination and is used in its imaginative capacity, e.g. a table becomes a house; a ball becomes a doll; a piece of Lego becomes a gun; jig-saw pieces become aeroplanes.

3 FANTASY PERSON PLAY

The child or other people participating change character in the child's imagination, e.g. the child becomes a cowboy; a baby; a dalek; a steam-engine; another child becomes any of the preceding people or objects.

4 IMMATERIAL FANTASY PLAY

The play includes fantasy people or objects which have no substantive identity in the environment, e.g. the child talks to non-existent people such as a co-pilot; feeds a non-existent horse; posts a non-existent letter in a non-existent post box.

It is arguable whether Piaget would include Representational Object Play as symbolic play. It is different from the other categories in that no transformation is required by the child. All the categories may be recorded concurrently. Consequently, a complex fantasy episode might necessitate sustained recording of all four categories or the three higher order categories, i.e. fantasy persons, fantasy objects and immaterial fantasy play, over several minutes. As with other behaviour categories, definitions and conventions are given in Appendix I. Other participants are recorded as taking part in the particular fantasy category when the subjects and their own behaviour showed this to be taking place. The categories therefore provide a measure of:

1 Complexity

2 Duration

3 Social participation

The categories are deliberately designed *not* to include any assessment of originality. In an extensive long-term study it might be possible to accord a measure of originality reliably, but in a study where a child is seen intensively for only one to two weeks, it is impossible for the observer to assess whether an apparently 'high original' role is, for instance, copied from the performance of a friend, or is in fact created by the child himself.

A Time spent in different types of fantasy play

Neither the number of children engaging in any type of fantasy play nor the length of time they spent in it varied significantly with social class, age or family position. Girls, however, spent significantly more time in fantasy person play than boys (see Table 6.1), although there was no variation in the number of children from either sex engaging in this type of fantasy play. Representational fantasy play occupied far more of the children's time than any of the other types of fantasy play (see Table 6.2).

Table 6.1   Mean percent of waking day spent in different forms of fantasy play

Fantasy Play	Mean % of Waking Day
Representational	9
Object	1
Person	1
Immaterial	1

Table 6.2   Mean number of intervals spent by boys and girls girls in fantasy person play

	Sex	Mean No. of Intervals	F Ratio	Level of Significance
Fantasy	m	6		
Person			7.01	P<0.01
Play	f	12		

B Time spent in complex fantasy play

Complex fantasy, where all three higher order fantasy categories were concurrent, i.e. involving fantasy object, person and immaterial fantasy play, was a rare event. A mean of 0.04 per cent of the waking day was spent in this way and the incidence of complex fantasy did not vary with any of the independent variables.

C The relationship between higher order fantasy play and other types of activity

Frequently the children engaged in other types of activity while fantasising, for example vehicle driving or water play. While the activity might be germane to the fantasy theme, we felt that the concurrent activity might be as important to the child as the fantasy element and also we wished to see which activities did accompany fantasisation. Therefore, when fantasy play occurred concurrently with another activity, both activities were recorded during that time interval. Dressing up and representational fantasy play were significantly the most likely categories to accompany the three higher order fantasy categories. Next came vehicle riding and listening to the radio or record player, which differed significantly from all other activities. There were no significant variations between any further activities (see Table 6.3).

Table 6.3   Time spent in higher order fantasy play as a percentage of total time spent in specific activities

Concurrent activity	% Accompanied by Higher Order Fantasy	Significance Levels between Proportions	
A Dressing up	16	A – B	NS
B Representational fantasy	14	B – C	P<0.001
C Vehicle riding	5		
D Listening to records/radio	5		
E All other activities	3	D – E	P<0.01

(Test for the difference between uncorrelated proportions, Guilford, 1965)

D The relationship between fantasy play and intelligence

Spearman Rank Order Correlation Co-efficients were computed between Standford Binet Intelligence Quotient Scores and

   i)   the total amount of time spent in each type of fantasy play, i.e. representational object play; fantasy object play; fantasy person play; immaterial fantasy play;

   ii) the amount of time spent in each of the above categories, when the child was playing on his own, with an adult, or with other children;

   iii) the amount of time spent in complex fantasy.

In no case were the measurements related either negatively or positively to Stanford-Binet IQ (P>0.05)

E The relationship between fantasy play and affect

Laughing, weeping and moaning were selected as behaviour categories likely to indicate the general level of 'happiness' or 'contentment' of the child. Spearman Rank Order correlation co-efficients were computed between the total incidence of each of these categories and the total incidence of any of the three higher order fantasy categories. The correlation co-efficients were not significant (P>0.05).

F The relationship between social participation and fantasy play

Since the literature suggests that parental participation in fantasy play encourages the child but the presence of other children may be disruptive to the privacy necessary to fantasy play, we computed the correlations between the incidence of fantasy play when there was either adult or child participation and the incidence when neither, adults nor children respectively, participated. Subjects who never engaged in the fantasy play being analysed were excluded. The incidence of the three higher order categories combined correlated significantly with increased adult participation. Representational fantasy play also showed a postive correlation but only at the 0.05 level of significance (see Table 6.4). Correlations between fantasy play incidence and the participation of other children were low and not significant.

Table 6.4   Pearson Product Moment correlations between incidence of fantasy play and adult and child participation in fantasy play

Fantasy Play	Adult Participation	Child Participation
Person, Object and Immaterial Fantasy	0.20 P<0.01	−0.03 NS
Representational Fantasy	0.17 P<0.03	0.02 NS

(Maximum N = 165)

It was feasible that the correlation between the amount of adult participation and fantasy play were merely due to the fact that if a child was spending more time in fantasy play there was more time when an adult might participate. If this were the case the same relationship should be true for other activities. Therefore, for all non-functional activities, excluding those which were dependent on the participation of another person, such as 'Being read to', correlations were computed between the incidence of that activity and adult participation. Again, for each specific activity, subjects who had never engaged in that activity were excluded from the analysis (see Table 6.5). A similar computation was done with the same activities in terms of child participation. Only five of the activities show a significant correlation between adult participation and incidence without adult participation. Where correlations were performed with child participation as one of the variables, vehicle riding and climbing, swinging and bouncing show significant correlations and ball play and spontaneous running and jumping give postitive correlations which are just short of significance at the 0.05 level (see Table 6.6).

Table 6.5 **Pearson Product Moment correlations between incidincidence of specific activities and incidence of those activities when an adult participated**

Activities	Adult Participation	Level of Participation
Looking at Books	0.22	$P<0.01$
Painting	0.37	$P<0.005$
Television Watching	0.20	$P<0.01$
Miniature Skilled Physical Activities	0.30	$P<0.005$
Animal Activities	0.21	$P<0.05$

(Maximum N = 165)

Table 6.6   Pearson Product Moment correlations between incidence of specific activities and incidence of those activities when another child participated

Activities	Child Participation	Level of Significance
Vehicle Riding and Driving	0.25	P<0.003
Climbing, Bouncing and Swinging	0.35	P<0.001

(Maximum N = 165)

The percentage of adults participating in fantasy play did not vary between social classes.

Discussion and conclusions

This study is an attempt to quantify fantasy in the children's natural surroundings. The findings here differ from the results obtained in preschool institutions, in that we have not found social class differences in either the total amount of any of the categories of fantasy play or in complex fantasy play. This suggests that class may be interacting with other variables in the institutional environments to produce the reported differences. In her model of play, Hutt (1979) suggests that children must be relaxed and at ease for ludic behaviour, which includes fantasy play, to take place. It is possible that in the Smilansky study *(op. cit.)* and later work comparing class differences in children's fantasy play, disadvantaged children are more stressed in the Kindergarten or Nursery School atmosphere, that this inhibits their ludic behaviour and therefore it is to be expected that they exhibit less fantasy play. Thus it may be that 'happy' children do fantasise more, but because only unless they are relaxed and happy are children capable of fantasy. Tizard *et al* (1976) considered that the working class children in their study were engaging in outdoor play to avoid Nursery Staff contact, which lends support to the idea that these children are not as confident and 'at home' in the preschool surroundings as their middle class counterparts. When children from low socio-economic backgrounds have become accustomed to school and are more confident in their surroundings, they might then be expected to participate in more fantasy play, especially out of doors, as Eifermann (1971) found.

If fantasy play gives rise to the development or benefits people have suggested and is more prevalent in middle class children, it seems surprising that no connection between IQ score and fantasy play has been established – a correlation which this study also failed to find. This seems a further argument that fantasy play is being suppressed in working class children in the preschool setting rather than that these children lack the ability to fantasise.

A great deal of the fantasy play observed was highly repetitive and stereotyped. The same play was performed repeatedly by individual children on different occasions and also different children would engage in very similar fantasisation. This was particularly true of representational fantasy play, where the boys spent long periods parking and reparking toy cars and the girls arranging and rearranging domestic replica objects. Representational fantasy play lent itself to the incorporation of higher order fantasy in that if no appropriate toy or piece of domestic apparatus was available, immaterial fantasisation would supply the necessary working ingredients or car park. Similarly, object play fantasisation could fill in deficiencies. Neither introduction necessarily meant the play had become more flexible and innovative.

Various fantasy person characters were enacted by a number of children. Their portrayal was stylised. Children usually announced that they were one of these characters and were going to 'play' the particular character. 'Batman' or 'Robin' were depicted by running head down and with arms outstretched behind; 'daleks' extended a stiff arm and growled in a monotone: 'Exterminate, exterminate'; 'Bionic Man' or 'Steve Austin' ran in slow motion with massive strides; 'Kung Fu' gave a Karate-type kick; Tarzan gave a Tarzan shout. Monsters growled with clawed fingers; ghosts haunted with spooky finger; stranglers went about their business in the conventional way. While children were never questioned about the identities of these roles, it was as though the small pieces of action which defined the character had become emancipated from the character itself and so possibly this was being passed on and imitated between

children, without them ever having seen the television programme
or comic strip. It was exceptional but not impossible for one of these
characters to go on and become involved in an adventure and por-
tray more varied behaviour.

More flexible and innovative role play appeared to occur when
the child took the part of someone with well defined occupational
activities, such as a doctor, nurse, teacher, fireman, policeman, bus
conductor, or, in one case, a striptease artiste. Family roles
appeared to function in a similar way where a child became a
Mummy, Daddy, Baby or Big Sister. Mummies cooked, cleaned
and went shopping, Daddies went to work and drove about in cars.
In the same way, children occasionally pretended to be what they were
in fact. Two little girls, for instance, became 'two little girls' going
shopping. Children also became particular individuals, several girls
becoming 'Mummy' as opposed to 'a Mummy', and a few boys similarly became their own fathers. Children would become an absent
friend or, occasionally, they would swap characters; this occasionally happened when parents were playing with children.

That adult participation in fantasy did stimulate the children to
increased fantasy play appears true. As neither child participation
nor adult participation in the majority of other types of activities
gave positive correlations with increase in those specific activities,
the possibility that the effect is merely one of increased time available for parental participation in a particular activity can be dis-
counted. Forms of adult participation varied: an adult sometimes
participated strictly under orders, as for instance when one boy prepared a 'car' with a record as a steering wheel, a hammer bench as
a seat and an Action Man as passenger. He invited his mother, who
was in the room: 'Come on, get in the car, we're going shopping',
and then arranged pieces of Lego to look like headlights and a car
bonnet at the front. He rebuilt the car to his satisification, mended
imaginary tools, installed a peg-board as a stereo set, and then
invited his mother again into the car: 'Come on Mum, get in the car'.

Mother: 'Where are we going?'

Child: 'We're going to Butlins'.

The mother was then provided with a kitchen chair on which to sit.
Various re-arrangements were made.

Child: 'I'm going on a boat, you sit in a deckchair,' A board and
box became the boat and then the child immediately announced:
'We're going home now' and everything turned back into the car.

The mother's role throughout had been to sit in the kitchen chair.

Incidence of very active participation was more rare. An exceptional case was an Only child, both of whose parents worked. Every morning, after the father had left, the mother would do her housework and then, at about 9.30am, an elderly gentleman who worked with the mother, would call to pick up her and her daughter, drop the daughter off to spend the day with her aunt and then take the mother on to where they worked. While the mother made him a cup of coffee, traditionally, every morning he would play with the child. Various dolls and soft toys were known as 'the Kids', and every morning the gentleman, the child and 'the Kids' would have some expedition. The morning of the observation, 'the Kids' went to hospital and were attended by a doctor and nurse, played by the elderly gentleman and the child. 'The Kids' were made to wait in hospital cubicles for their turn and given medical examinations with a cup as a stethescope and injections from the Lego tray as a medicine chest, with a paint brush hypodermic needle. Examination and diagnoses appeared to be more the province of the nurse than the doctor on this occasion.

Shopping expeditions were occasionally the setting for adult/child fantasy games. Participants took the roles of customers and various types of shopkeepers and bought and sold relevant goods. Occasionally an adult would engineer a situation by means of fantasisation to make a joke with the child. For example, one father had just received his new Heavy Goods Vehicle Licence. He gave his daughter the old, expired licence and then invited her, clutching it, to get on her bicycle. She immediately obliged and was arrested by a 'policeman' for driving with an out of date licence. At other times a well intentioned remark from an adult appeared to be regarded as an intrusion into a private matter and terminated fantasy play. A child, who was a keen follower of the 'Lone Ranger' on television, found an old broom stave and tatty piece of string in the back yard. She tied the string to the top of the handle and then galloped up and down talking to the stick as 'Silver', the Lone Ranger's horse, and to herself in the person of the Lone Ranger. Her mother, who was in earshot in the kitchen, came out to hang some washing on the line and said cheerfully:

'Are you the Lone Ranger?'

'No.'

'Who are you then?'

'Mister Nobody.'
and the fantasy ceased until the mother had returned indoors.

When the other activities which increased significantly with adult participation are examined, it is apparent that they are activities which all necessitate adult initiation, participation and guidance. Arguably, a small child does not become interested in books until an adult has shown him what they contain. Painting requires considerable adult assistance to get the painting started and maintained, as mentioned in the last chapter. Television watching is discussed in the next chapter, but the children's attention spans were usually very brief. Interest was engaged and sustained when adults drew children's attention to aspects of a programme or expanded what was shown in a way which was meaningful to the child. 'Miniature skilled physical games' were by definition skilled and the child needed to be shown how to play them and required the guidance and participation of an older child or adult to maintain the game. A major portion of 'Animal activities' was domestic pet care and again this involved adult guidance or demonstration. This suggests that where adults participate in fantasy play, the activity has common characteristics shared with the constructive and cognitively stimulating aspect of the activities described above. In contrast, the activities which were stimulated by child participation were vigorous, physical, and unrestrained activities.

This increased fantasy person play found among the girls in this study contrast with Emmerich's (1971) finding that in preschool settings, boys engaged in more fantasy activity than girls. There seem to be several plausible reasons to account for this discrepancy; while girls enacted conventional male roles, boys did not enact conventional female roles; in the home more potential female models were available than male models. It therefore may be that girls were more stimulated by the domestic setting than the boys. As the roles which were based on reality (as opposed to those based on television or comic strip characters) produced the most flexible and extensive fantasy play, this factor may again be enhancing the girls' role play in the domestic setting. Props suitable for domestic fantasy are also more readily available at home.

The activities which occurred most frequently with fantasy play showed some sexual variation. Dressing up, which occurred most frequently with higher order fantasy play, was indulged in far more by the girls, vehicle riding was a male activity, while representational fantasy play and listening to records and the radio did not show sex differences in terms of the amount of time spent on them. Intuition and tradition suggest that dressing up encourages fantasy play and props and clothes are frequently provided in Nursery Schools for this purpose. Children spent very little time listening to the radio or records but fantasy occurred when songs or music indicated an animal or, for instance, a train part.

Permanent imaginary companions were extremely rare. In the pilot study, one three-year-old girl started attributing the character 'Mandy' to a variety of objects. For example, her mother took the child and her brother for a walk and the children prevailed on her to carry a ball so that they could have a game during the walk. They had their game and their mother suggested leaving the ball behind and collecting it on the way home; tears and a temper tantrum ensued 'You can't leave Mandy behind'. A three-and-a-half-year-old boy kept up running conversations to himself and at times seemed to address someone called 'ducks'. The observer asked his mother about 'ducks' and she said that she had not been able to work it out: he frequently, when he thought he was not being over-heard, had conversations including 'ducks', but there was no further evidence that 'ducks' existed. The only other case of an imaginary companion was that of another three-and-a-half-year-old, a girl, who referred to a 'Ghost' who lived upstairs, and this worried her mother. On an evening observation when the child was being dried on her mother's lap, after her bath, she said happily 'When I go to bed, Ghost will be there.' Her mother said rather sharply, 'Nonsense, there's no ghost upstairs', and the child replied 'Yes there is, he's lovely; he goes to bed with me'. None of these subjects were Only children and the low incidence of 'imaginary companions' might suggest that when they do occur they are very memorable and delightful to parents and that therefore in recollection the latter tend to overemphasise their occurrence.

Thus fantasy play, apart from representational fantasy play, was infrequent. It should be borne in mind that when studies are made in preschool settings, 'free play' periods are normally chosen as the periods for observation, therefore biasing the sample time towards the recording of fantasy play, compared with the child's behaviour throughout the entire school day. Whereas fantasy play tuition has been shown to increase aspects of the child's behaviour directly related to fantasy play, specific additional benefical developments have not been fully established and it seems premature to emphasise the need for fantasy play to be 'taught' in schools. Indeed, both Klinger (1971) and Hutt (1979) have postulated that fantasy play in children is the precursor of day dreamings in adults. Singer (1961) found that fantasy play increased a child's ability to wait, in other words to fill in a time lacking external stimulation. Arguably, encouraging fantasy play in early childhood might increase day dreaming in later school life. That children enjoy social fantasy play is undeniable. It is an activity that is highly dependent on verbal communication among the participants. We would therefore suggest that it is one of a range of teaching tools which can be used to engage the child's interest and encourage verbal communication.

Chapter 7
Television, radio and record playing

This study provided a unique opportunity to assess by direct observation the amount of television watching by preschool children. Estimates of television watching for preschool children are generally based on parental estimates. Lyle and Hoffman (1972) estimated from parental interviews that preschool children watched between 23 and 33 hours a week of television programmes. However, Bechtel, Achelpohl and Ackers (1972) demonstrated that people tended to overestimate their own viewing time by 25 – 50 per cent too much.

We recorded when the child was actually watching television, assessed in terms of visual attention to the screen. In the pilot study we attempted to differentiate between active and passive watching, as so many preschool programmes suggest that children should join in with a song, a mime or by answering questions. Very few children made any overt response to this type of overture and it seemed an invalid assessment of the child's concentration on the programme. It was impossible to differentiate between a child watching apparently intently and a child watching in a similar way but whose mind was wandering. We also thought a measurement of the total time the television was on would be of interest. We found we could not reliably assess when the child could potentially either see or hear the television and so we eventually classified the television as 'on' when the child was in the house and the set was switched on. This was easy to apply and therefore reliable and valid in that the television was potentially available to the child to view if he wished. (In the majority of homes the child could hear the television all the time it was on, even if upstairs and unable to see it.) In addition, where identifiable, the programme the child was watching was recorded.

In the pilot study we had very little time spent by children in listening to the radio or record players and we therefore placed them both in the same category. We have recorded when the child was listening to the radio or a record, assessed by his overt behaviour, and also, as with television, when either of these was on when the child was in the house.

A Time spent watching television

Only 8 per cent of the sample never watched television at all during the course of observation. The children spent an average 9 per cent of their time watching television, which, calculated in terms of a twelve hour waking day and making no distinction between week days and Saturdays and Sundays, is 65 minutes per day. There were no differences in total time spent watching television according to class, sex, age or family position. The majority of the time the children watched television on their own, adults spending an average of 7 minutes watching programmes with the child in an active and positive way. Again the amount of time adults spent watching television with children did not vary according to the independent variables.

B The time the television was 'on' in the home

Television sets were 'on' and available to the children for a far greater time than the children actually spent watching television. Despite the fact that working class children watched the same amount of television as the middle class children, the sets were on a great deal more in the working class homes; expressed in terms of percentage of the children's waking day, this was 29 per cent and 38 per cent respectively, a significant difference.

Table 7.1 Mean time the television was 'on' per waking day

Social Class	'Time On'	F Ratio	Level of Significance
MC	3 hrs 27 mins		
		9.72	P<0.005
WC	4 hrs 37 mins		

C Time spent in listening to the radio and records

This activity occupied very little of the children's time, less than a minute of the total time observed, when averaged across the entire sample. Children may have been listening to, for instance, the radio in a way which was not overtly detectable while they engaged in other activities. As mentioned, radio and record listening was not recorded differentially but the majority of the measurable listening was to records specifically played for the children's benefit, such as Nursery Rhyme records or Mary Poppins. Although radio programmes were not recorded, the majority of programmes were from Radio 2 and occasionally the local station. At no time did any child listen to Radio 4's 'Listen with Mother', which was running throughout the course of the study, or the local radio station's equivalent programme for preschool children.

D Total time when radios and records were 'on' in the home

The total time radio and records were on was mainly composed of radio time. This did not vary at all between groups and averaged 17 per cent of the children's waking day, or exactly two hours.

E Television programmes watched

As data collection in the main study extended over 3½ years, television programmes changed over this period. Some programmes were dropped by the networks and new programmes were introduced. A total of 234 programmes were seen at some time by at least one of the children. Some of these programmes were seen extremely briefly for perhaps only one or two thirty second time intervals. Where possible, the programme seen was checked against the advertised schedule for identification.

The programmes watched by two or more children are listed in Table 7.2. However, given the problem of programme change, it was more meaningful to group the programmes according to content and then examine the types of programme the children were choosing to watch in terms of viewing time. The first column of Table 7.2 indicates the way individual programmes were classified in Table

7.3, e.g. 'Play School' was classified as 16, 'Small children's programmes'. Commercial classifications made by the BBC or IBA were
too global for our purposes. Our classification differentiates between different types of adult programmes such as adventure stories
where physical activity, car chases, etc. are likely to take place, and
adult drama with domestic and non-violent themes. All advertisements and programme lists were classified together but separated
from trailers. All cartoons were placed in one category except the
cartoons specifically designed for small children. Table 7.4 gives a
listing of all small children's programmes viewed, grouped according to content or type of production.

The programmes specifically designed for small children
occupied the greatest proportion of the subjects' viewing time; of
these 'Play School' was watched by the greatest number of children,
followed by 'You and Me', 'Rainbow' and 'Blue Peter'. Often the
children watched programmes for very short periods and we considered that the time the children spent in sustained watching of a
programme without diverting their attention to another activity
could be taken as an indication of their interest. These bout lengths
were calculated as means of the median bout length for individual
children for specific programme types and are presented on Table
7.3. The mean bout length is greatest for 'Small children's programmes'. While the total time spent watching advertisements is the second highest percentage of total viewing time, the mean bout length
while watching cartoons is comparatively long.

To assess when children were watching television, we calculated
the number of programmes seen at particular times, to the nearest
hour. Viewing extended from 8.00am to 8.00pm (Breakfast television had not started showing during the study.) Viewing began to
rise at 10.00am, peaking at 12.00 and then declining during the
afternoon to peak again suddenly at 4.00pm and 5.00pm, the
maximum viewing times. The children continued to watch, but to a
lesser extent at 6.00pm and 7.00pm and then the figures fall rapidly
as the children were put to bed.

Discussion and conclusions

The children were observed to watch less television than has previously been estimated from parental reports. However, television

Table 7.2 Number of children who watched specific programmes, in rank order

Programme Type (see Table 7.3)	Programme	No.of Children	Programme Type (see Table 7.3)	Programme	No.of Children
7	Advertisements	93	3	Ghost Busters	3
16	Play School	60	3	Happy Ever After	3
4	News	34	16	Isi Noho	3
8	Programme Trailers	19	3	It 'aint 'alf 'ot, Mum	3
2	Crossroads	18	2	Little House on the Prairie	3
9	Test Cards	17	1	Lone Ranger	3
16	You and Me	14	3	Man About the House	3
16	Rainbow	12	5	Mr and Mrs	3
4	ATV Today	11	2	The Sullivans	3
14	Blue Peter	11	4	Today's People	3
12	Top of the Pops	10	16	Trumpton	3
4	Nationwide	10	2	The Waltons	3
5	Pebble Mill	9	13	Watch	3
16	Pipkin	9	16	Andy Pandy	2
16	Paper Play	8	16	Bagpuss	2
16	Mr Trimble	8	16	Camberwick Green	2
16	Jackanory	7	14	Crackerjack	2
2	Coronation Street	6	11	Deputy Dawg	2
14	Magpie	6	4	First Report	2
12	Animal Kwackers	5	5	Good Afternoon	2
3	Happy Days	5	11	The Great Grape Ape	2
5	Opportunity Knocks	5	16	Handful of Songs	2
16	Rupert Bear	5	13	How	2
16	Sooty	5	13	John Craven's Newsround	2
16	Stepping Stones	5	6	Kitchen Garden	2
4	Tomorrow's World	5	16	Little Blue (2)	2
16	Wombles	5	16	Mary, Mungo and Midge	2
3	Dave Allen and Friends	4	4	Olympic Games	2
2	Emmerdale Farm	4	14	Potty Time	2
16	Hickory House	4	11	Scooby Doo	2
16	Mumfie	4	1	Space 1999	2
16	Words and Pictures	4	1	Star Trek	2
10	Survival	4	16	Teddy Edward	2
2	Angels	3	15	Time Tunnel	2
16	Bod	3	11	Boss Cat	2
15	Chorlton and the Wheelies	3	12	The Arrows	2
2	General Hospital	3			

A further 161 individual programmes were watched, each by one child only.

Table 7.3   Television

Programme Type	Number of Individual Programmes	Total Time Watched (Minutes)	Mean Bout Length (Minutes)	Time Watched as a % of Total Viewing Time
1 Adventure; Science Fiction Detective; Cowboy:	23	231	3.3	4
2 Adult drama, Non-adventure based:	25	482	1.9	9
3 Adult Comedy	25	254	2.6	5
4 Outside and Sporting Events; Adult Documentaries; News:	30	298	1.3	5
5 Adult Quizzes; Competitions; Magazine Programmes:	12	137	1.8	3
6 Adult Education:	6	31	1.5	1
7 Advertisements:	N/A	536	1.6	10
8 Programme Trailers:	N/A	43	1.5	1
9 Test Cards:	N/A	27	1.1	1
10 Animal Programmes:	3	35	1.8	1
11 Cartoons (Excluding Small Children's Cartoons):	37	339	4.6	6
12 Pop Music; Singing:	10	198	3.0	4
13 Schools; Children's Educational; Children's Documentaries	13	338	2.4	6
14 Children's Magazine Programmes; Quizzes; Competitions:	11	148	1.8	3
15 Children's Drama	35	219	2.6	4
16 Small Children's Programmes:	50	2207	5.1	40

N/A - Not Appropriate

Table 7.4   Small children's programmes

NARRATED STORY WITH STILL PICTURES
Jackanory   Story
Summer Story

STRING PUPPETS
Andy Pandy

ACTOR WITH PUPPETS
Mr Trimble   Sooty
Pipkin

ANIMATED MODELS WITH NARRATED STORY
Barnaby   Teddy Edward
Camberwick Green   The Weebles
Chigley   The Wombles
Hickory House   The Woozies
King Wilbur   The Laughing Policeman
Magic Roundabout   The Flumps
Noddy   Trumpton
Rupert Bear

CARTOONS
Bagpuss   Lippy Lion
Bod   Little Blue
Charlie's Climbing Tree   Mary, Mungo and Midge
Here Comes Mumfie   Mr Tickle
Isi Noho   Paddington Bear
Jamie and the Magic Torch   Roobarb

MAGAZINE PROGRAMMES
Fingerbobs   Piano Play Round
Handful of Songs   Play School
Over the Moon   Rainbow
Paper Play

EDUCATIONAL PROGRAMMES DESIGNED FOR SMALL CHILDREN
Heads and Tails   Stepping Stones
How Do You Do?   Words and Pictures
Sesame Street   You and Me

viewing did occupy a substantial part of the children's waking day and was the single activity on which the children spent most time. Individual variation in time spent watching television was high but did not vary consistently with either social class or age, which we had anticipated. What is interesting is that the children's actual viewing time did not reflect the time the television was 'on' and available to them and in this case there was a substantial social class difference. Given that the time adults spent actively watching television with the children did not vary between social classes, it may be that this type of adult participation is necessary to engage and sustain young children's interest. This is borne out by the analysis presented in Chapter 7, where television watching is one of the activities stimulated significantly by adult participation.

As we have mentioned, the programme changes made during the course of the study made the rating of a specific programme's popularity unreliable. Similarly the duration and frequency of presentation within the week distorts the picture. 'Play School' was undeniably popular with children in the sample but it was the only 'Small children's programme' to run throughout the study and to be shown twice a day, every weekday. Both mothers and children did try out ideas suggested by the 'Play School' presenters. The programme abounds with exciting and innovative ideas for making simple models and toys out of easily obtainable materials, such as paper and domestic junk. However, two working class mothers did specifically express their disapproval to the observers concerning 'Play School's' suggestions about messy play with paint. As one of them put it:

'Fancy a grown man showing a child how to splash with his feet in paint',

her son having immediately emulated the foot painting he had just seen to the detriment of the sitting room carpet. Similarly, advertisements appear on the Independent Television channel throughout the day and at frequent intervals; advertisements are short, snappy and frequently accompanied by a jingle which a child can soon identify. Children were seen to be sitting on the floor engaged in some other activity and on hearing a commercial's tune, they would look up, watch the television while the advertisement lasted, and then go back to their own activity.

Children and their parents were well aware of the scheduling of 'Small children's programmes' and the rise in the viewing in the morning coincides with the incidence of 'Small children's programmes'. Test card viewing usually occurred in the morning when a child anticipated the onset of these programmes. Both late morning and early afternoon scheduling of 'Small children's programmes' seemed to suit families' routines, mothers being able to begin preparing lunch after their morning's housework, while children watched television and similarly television provided a diversion for teatime preparation and when older children returned from school. The apparent popularity of domestic dramas such as 'Crossroads' and 'Coronation Street' was because they are scheduled in the early evening, more than once a week and they ran throughout the study and were followed by a number of the parents.

As none of the subjects ever listened to the 'Small children's programmes' available on the radio, it would appear that television has taken over completely in terms of small children's entertainment and radio was functioning merely as background noise. Allowing for time when both radio and television were on concurrently, it meant that the children were bathed in this type of background noise for five to six hours a day.

In our experience in the pilot study, where mothers had kept diaries of their children's days, they frequently recorded television watching as occupying a half hour period. When subsequently observing these children, it was noticeable that, although sitting near the television, when it was on they in fact only watched for a few fragmented time intervals, although it was easy to see why their parents had reported this type of occasion as television watching. This fits with the findings of Bechtel *et al.*, (1972) who reported that viewing is often overestimated.

While television is undoubtedly a boon to parents in terms of occupying demanding and active small children, as with most small children's activities, parental participation and intervention increases its potential for stimulation and interest. To adult eyes the 'Small children's programmes' available are excellent, offering varied, eye-catching and stimulating entertainment. As many of the programmes use a dialogue and attempt to incorporate the child, asking him questions and suggesting he joins in with songs and mimes and yet children were rarely seen to respond, it would be interesting to examine this aspect of presentation in detail experimentally. To determine, for example, if a child does not respond, whether this type of exhortation detracts from the child's interest and therefore comprehension of the programme. Where television progammes are used in Nursery Schools or Day Nurseries, staff should be aware that their participation in the viewing is important.

Chapter 8
Language

While a detailed analysis of the children's verbal experience in the home was beyond the scope of this research project, development of language is of such importance to the young child that we decided to measure selected aspects of speech which we considered to be of particular interest. In the pilot study we experimented with various measurements and found that if we were to restrict ourselves to a categorisation based on immediate, on-the-spot observer decisions recorded on the check-list, the number of potential items must inevitably be circumscribed to achieve an acceptable standard of reliability. We ruled out the use of radio microphones and tape recording speech for a number of reasons: the tape recording itself added another potential variable mitigating against the habituation of the child and his family to the observer and the observational process; children were deliberately unconstrained and a child wearing a radio-microphone attached to a jerkin would have presented problems in some out-of-doors situations and, for instance, while dressing and being bathed. The transcription and analysis of such recordings would also have been prohibitive in terms of analysis time. Therefore we selected a small number of specific measurements which we considered were of theoretical importance.

We felt that a measurement of the total amount of speech exchanged by the subject with both adults and children with whom he had contact was essential. We therefore recorded all speech between the subject and other people, identifying the speech recipient, and defined his general speech as:

Communication – any form of speech except moaning or aggressive speech to another individual.

We recorded separately:

Auto-talk – the subject talking to himself.

Singing – singing, humming and whistling.

Telephone – telephone talking.

We thought it would be interesting to see how auto-talk related to the amount of general social communication. Would high levels of communication to and from a child increase his 'chattiness' and therefore increase the probability of his talking to himself, or, conversely, do children talk to themselves in the absence of social communication? Singing, humming and whistling were combined as they occurred at low levels in the pilot study. Telephone talking was recorded separately because, although a rare event in the pilot study, it seemed a particularly potent experience to the children when it did occur and should not be included in any general communication. We thought that, given the difference in telephone ownership, the middle class children were more likely to take part in this activity than the working class children.

Speech was time sampled, but, unlike other behaviour categories, a one-zero time sampling convention was used, i.e. if speech occurred during an interval it was recorded as present. This was because the time sampling convention of estimating the preponderant length within the individual time interval is inappropriate to a behaviour such as speech, which cannot be taken as a state, Altmann (1974). While event recording in terms of utterances is only feasible with recorded material, this time sampling convention was used with all the speech categories.

In addition to the speech categories just described were the qualitative measures designed to tap areas of particular theoretical significance. In the Introduction we briefly outlined Bernstein's (1961) original formulation of his very influential linguistic theory. Later he presented a reformulation of his theory. He considers that:

'Universalistic meanings are those in which principles and generalisations are made linguistically implicit'. Bernstein (1975) and goes on to argue that 'elaborated codes' orient thier users to universalistic meanings, 'restricted codes' to particularistic meanings, that

'One of the aspects of the class system is to limit access to elaborated codes'. Bernstein (1975)

Rather than his earlier position of suggesting that code use dichotomises along middle and working class lines, he now considers that language must be examined in different contexts and the predominant use, exposed in these contexts, can assign the subject to having access to a particular code. The contexts Bernstein specifies are:

1 The regularitive context.
2 The instructional context.
3 The imaginative or innovative context.
4 The inter-personal context.

Arguably, our sample of a 'normal' day in the life of the child covers the four contexts. We therefore defined two categories, 'instructions' and 'abstracts':

Instructions:
– giving of information, which may be used outside the child's own home (i.e. excluding specific localised events) which does not involve elaboration or expansion of a concept, such as specifically naming objects by drawing the child's attention to them, making statements of fact without justification, correcting the child's speech to the individual's own speech criteria.

The exclusion of 'specific localised events' refers to statements concerning the child's own home, such as 'No, that's Daddy's mug'. Simple labelling frequently took the form of naming objects, animals, etc. For example:

Mother, to child looking at a book on African mammals:
'What's that? It's an elephant.'

Colour and letter naming and counting were all frequent sources of instructions:

Mother, supervising the distribution of wine gums:
'No, that's not a red one; it's orange.'

Mother and child looking at a book together:
'Here's P for Paul' (child's name).

Mother, to child fetching cutlery while helping her mother lay the table:
'Look, you've only got two forks, one, two,' (pointing at the forks) 'get another one, that's right, one, two, three'.

When parents were correcting children's speech, some corrections were straightforward and accepted syntactic corrections, e.g.

Child, pointing at the television screen at a film of sheepdog trials:
'Look at the sheeps!'

Mother:
'Sheep, not sheeps.'

However, parents also corrected their children to their own criteria of what is socially acceptable and we felt here that this should be included, although it was impossible to match these against accepted external criteria. For example:

> Child, shouting back to her Mother, who has called from the kitchen:
> 'What?' (from the living room)
> Mother, coming into living room:
> 'Don't say 'What?', say 'Pardon'.'

We also wanted to record when information of a more complex form was given to the child and we therefore included a second category of what we termed abstract explanations.

Abstracts:
– statements or questions which involve abstractions to a class of individuals, objects or events, i.e. which includes a general principle.

While 'Instructions' did not include any justification of the label or information, 'Abstracts' did so. For example:

> Child, watching her mother plug in and then switch on the hoover, which began to hum:
> 'Why does it do that?'
> Mother:
> 'Well, the electricity makes it go; it comes down this wire' (pointing to the hoover flex) 'and into the hoover, like with my mixer when I plug that in and switch it on; the electricity makes that go. It's very complicated and I don't understand quite how.'

Or,

> Mother and daughter watching an archeological television programme, archeologist squatting and holding a skull in his hand, expounding on the particular form of early man to whom it had belonged; child:
> 'What's that'?
> Mother:
> 'A skull, it's somebody's head, who has been dead a very, very long time and buried in the earth.'
> Child, pausing for thought:
> 'When you're ill, Jesus makes you better, doesn't he?'
> Mother:
> 'Yes.'

Child:
'Who kills you then?'

We used two categories and recorded when the child was given either an 'Instruction' or an 'Abstract'. In the previous example, 'What's that?' would be coded as demand for an instruction as there is nothing explicit in the question for more than a simple instructional reply, i.e. 'A skull.' Predominantly, it is the respondent who controls the conversation and can extend the reply to abstract form. However, 'Why does it do that?' and 'Who kills you then?' cannot be replied to in the form of a straightforward label and were therefore coded as demands for an 'Abstract'. Consequently demands for 'Abstracts' are very rare, usually taking the form of a demand for an 'Instruction' and then it is the parent who expands and gives an 'Abstract' in response.

We predicted according to Bernstein's theory that middle class children would receive far more 'Abstracts' than the working class group and that they would demand more. We predicted that there would be a similar difference in the number of 'Instructions' the social class groups received, but that this would not show so wide a difference.

An aspect of communication which we also considered would be important in guiding and changing the child's behaviour, sustaining his interest in an outgoing activity or suggesting a new one, was what we classified as an 'Option'. An 'Option' was:

Option:
– an invitation, a suggestion to the subject that he does something – includes non-verbal communication.

'Options' related only to non-functional activities, i.e. excluding such activities as toileting and eating. They allowed the child an element of choice and did not include commands or directives which the child was explicitly expected to obey. For example, a mother had been washing the kitchen floor and the child, having been forbidden access to the kitchen while this was going on, was getting bored with being on his own in the sitting room.

Mother, coming in: 'Go and get your Mister Man book and I'll read it to you while the floor's drying.'

'Options' also frequently extended or expanded an activity in which the child was engaged:

Mother: 'Why don't you give teddy a paddle too?' (to her nude child splashing about in paddling pool in garden).'We can dry him off afterwards.'

We included here non-verbal 'Options', which occurred occasionally. A conversation between an adult and child might have laid the basis for some future activity and the final signal might be a hand held out to the child indicating that now the adult was ready for them to go off to do their particular activity. We also scored when the child rejected an 'Option' given by someone else. This frequently took the form of ignoring the invitation and here again non-verbal communication was included. Similarly, we recorded 'Options' extended from the subject to other people and when these were rejected. For example:

Child, attempting to stick coloured stars on a piece of paper in a particular pattern: 'Mummy, come and help me.'

Mother: 'No, I'm too busy', (continuing to bustle about the kitchen).

We predicted, on the basis of Bernstein's (1973) distinction between two modes of control, the imperative mode of control and the mode based upon appeals, that middle class parents would be more likely to use 'Options' than working class parents.

While being unable to make a detailed categorisation of the broad area of affective speech because of the practical constraints of the reseach, we distinguished two categories:

Negative speech: direct verbal punishment and aggression and threats.

Positive speech: approval, praise, affection and promise of treats.

Thus 'Negative' speech would include instances of direct verbal punishment such as curtailment of the child's immediate activities:

Mother, to child who was constantly watched from the kitchen window while he played in the garden, tapping on the kitchen window and shouting angrily:

'You put that down!' (outdoor brush) 'I've told you, it's dirty, put it down.'

Or:

Mother, to four-year-old, eldest, daughter, who was attempting to kiss the six-week-old baby being cuddled on her mother's knee:

'Get away, I am not having *you* kiss her.'

Threats could be grounded in reality or be mythical, although presumably indistinguishable to the child. For example:

A child was watching her mother change her six-month-old baby brother, when the baby suddenly grabbed a piece of paper from his sister which she had been holding. She riposted by lurching forward to poke him in the face and the mother speedily interceded, saying:

'Jane, if you ever do that I'll smack you.'

Or:

Mother, finding child soaking wet yet again, having dragged a kitchen chair over to the sink and dabbled under the tap:

'Oh, you're naughty; I'm going to get a policeman to take you away.'

Or:

Mother, repeatedly, two weeks before Christmas, when a child was about to commit a misdemeanour:

'Santa'll bring a bag of cinders.'

Or:

Mother, with shift working husband asleep upstairs. She had previously explained to the observer that he was never woken by the children's noise during the day when he was sleeping:

'You'll wake your Dad, and then he'll be down'.

At the other end of the affective scale we distinguished 'Positive' speech. This included admiration of a child's activity or completed puzzle, or praise for some domestic chore, for example:

Mother, to child descending from a chair by the kitchen sink after washing up the dinner plates:

'You're a good little washer-up.'

We also included promise of reward for good behaviour:

'You've been a good boy' (during the morning's housework)

'we'll go to the swings after dinner.'

Again, we predicted class differences, the middle class being expected to use less 'Negative' speech and more 'Positive' speech than the working class parents.

We were also interested in whether particular activities were accompanied by more speech than others and whether instructional and abstract speech categories occurred concurrently with some activities more than others.

Evidence for sex differences in early language development is variable. McCarthy (1954) considered that girls had a slight advantage in all aspects of language development and Terman and Tyler (1954) came to the same conclusion. Maccoby and Jacklin (1974) consider that girls' verbal abilities mature somewhat earlier in life than boys'. However, Fairweather (1976) and MacCauley (1977) consider there is no evidence for female superiority in language development. MacDonald (in preparation), in a very detailed review of the different stages of early language acquisition, points out that some of the discrepancies can be explained by showing that the evidence for female advantage only exists on specific dimensions and that the advantage is only held for a short space of time before the males catch up. For example, girls appear to score higher on mean length of utterances (MLU) until the age of three years, but after this MLU is probably an inappropriate measure and possibly sex differences are only discernible using an upper band measure. Vocabulary acquisition appears to be faster in girls until the age of three years, while with aural comprehension no female advantage is found after four years of age. With grammar acquisition and language complexity the effects last longer, girls performing with superiority until the age of seven years. The evidence for increased female loquacity at any time is dubious.

On the measure used in this study very subtle differences in language production will not be discernible. However, a question which needs answering in the literature is whether the female language advantages which have been substantiated are due to biological maturity or increased verbal interaction between adults and the girls. Lewis (1969; 1972) suggests that infant girls are more vocally responsive to human faces and to their mothers' vocal and tactile stimulation than boys. If there are sex differences in vocal and verbal interaction we would predict girls scoring higher on general speech, both to and from adults but particularly from mothers, and that girls would demand and receive more abstracts and instructions.

Finally, the Stanford-Binet Intelligence test scores are reported in this chapter, as the majority of the test items depend on both verbal and cognitive abilities and these results will be discussed with reference to information from previous chapters.

A General speech to and from the child

Speech from the subject to adults did not vary with social class, age or sex, but showed differences according to family position. Only children spoke more to adults than either Eldest or Youngest children and Eldest children more than Youngest, i.e. Youngest children were having least general conversation with adults. A similar pattern emerges when speech specifically to either parent is examined. In particular, Youngest children talked much less to their fathers than did either of the other two groups. Where speech to other children is concerned, the situation reverses: Youngest subjects spoke far more to other children than either of the other two groups and Eldest more than Only children (see Table 8.1)

Speech from other people to the subject showed a similar pattern to expressed speech (see Table 8.2). Again, there was no difference between groups according to social class, sex or age, although adult speech did tend to decline with age, but family position exerted an influence. Only children were talked to by adults far more than either of the other two groups, but Eldest children did receive more adult speech than Youngest. The Only/Youngest difference was maintained when maternal speech was considered in isolation. Fathers spoke more to Only and Eldest children and least to Youngest children. As with the subject's speech to other children, child speech to subject reverses the adult pattern.

Youngest children received most speech from other children. While in the adult speech categories adults speak to the subject in more intervals than the subject speaks to them, in the 'between child' speech categories the Eldest and the Only children spend a greater number of intervals speaking to the other children compared to receiving their speech. In contrast, the Youngest children speak to other children in fewer intervals than they are spoken to by other children (see Tables 8.1 and 8.2).

B Moaning and whining; telephone talk and singing

Moaning and whining, overall, showed a tendency to decline with age, but this effect just did not approach significance at the 0.05 level. Telephone speech was extremely rare over all the groups and showed no variation between them. Singing, on the other hand, varied with sex, and the girls sang more than the boys (see Table 8.3).

Table 8.1 Speech from the subject to other people

Person Receiving Speech	Family Position	Mean No. of Intervals	F Ratio	Significance Level	Scheffé Comparisons
All adults	Eldest	303			O v. E P<0.05
	Only	355	20.0	P<0.001	Y v. O P<0.01
	Youngest	236			Y v. E P<0.01
Mother	Eldest	236			
	Only	256	4.4	P<0.01	
	Youngest	195			
Father	Eldest	47			Y v. E P<0.1
	Only	52	6.1	P<0.005	Y v. O P<0.01
	Youngest	24			
Children	Eldest	96			E v. O P<0.01
	Only	60	7.9	P<0.001	Y v. O P<0.01
	Youngest	121			Y v. E P<0.01

(Scheffé comparisons omitted from Table were non-significant)

Table 8.2 Speech to the subject from other people

Person Speaking	Family Position	Mean No. of Intervals	F Ratio	Significance Level	Scheffé Comparisons
Adults	Eldest	333			Y v. E P<0.01
	Only	390	16.6	P<0.001	O v. E P<0.05
	Youngest	275			Y v. O P<0.01
Mother	Eldest	263			
	Only	289	3.4	P<0.05	Y v. O P<0.05
	Youngest	229			
Father	Eldest	54			Y v. E P<0.05
	Only	59	5.5	P<0.005	Y v. O P<0.05
	Youngest	229			
Children	Eldest	72			Y v. E P<0.01
	Only	56	11.2	P<0.001	Y v. O P<0.01
	Youngest	124			

(Scheffé comparisons omitted from Table were non-significant)

Table 8.3 Singing

Behaviour	Sex	Mean	F Ratio	Level of Significance
Singing	m	12	8.20	P<0.005
	f	20		

C Auto-talk

Auto-talk occupied, on the basis of an average across all the subjects, 10 per cent of all intervals observed. It showed no variation with any of the four independent variables. It seemed surprising that auto-talk did not differ according to family position. We had anticipated that Only children, compensating for their lack of chatter with other children, would produce more. To see if some children were generally 'chattier' than others, we performed a Pearson Product-moment Correlation between auto-talk and the subject's social talk to and from other people. We separated adult and child talk because of the previously demonstrated family position differences. We postulated that significant positive correlations would indicate that 'chatty' children talk both to other people and to themselves more than other children.

Table 8.4 Pearson Product-moment correlation coefficients between auto-talk and social speech variables

	Auto-talk	Social Speech from Subject	Adult Talk to Subject
Social Speech from Subject	−0.32 P<0.001		
Adult Talk to Subject	−0.20 P<0.001	0.60 P<0.001	
Child Talk to Subject	0.20 P<0.01	0.14 NS	−0.51 P<0.001

However, Table 8.4 shows that auto-talk and social speech from the subject are significantly negatively related, as is auto-talk with adult and child speech to the subject. While adult speech is positively correlated with social talk from the subject, adult and child speech to the subject are negatively correlated. This suggested that children were talking to themselves when social speech opportunities were lacking. To clarify this we performed a partial correlation between auto-talk and the subject's social speech, controlling for both adult and child speech to the subject. The negative correlation reduces to 0.03 (NS), confirming that auto-talk occurred in the absence of social speech.

D 'Instructions' and 'Abstracts'

Ninety-three per cent of the children received instructional speech from an adult in the course of the observation. The mean number of intervals when this occurred is slightly higher for the middle class children compared with the working class children, but the difference does not approach significance. Demands for 'Instructions' did vary with social class, the middle class asking for more from adults; demands for 'Instructions', but not 'Instructions' from adults, also varied significantly with family position (see Table 8.5). Only children demanded more 'Instructions' from adults than either Eldest or Youngest children. Only 17 per cent of the sample received, and 9 per cent demanded, 'Instructions' from other children. While the differences do not approach significance, it was the Youngest children who were both demanding and receiving most.

Abstract explanations were only given to 15 per cent of the children; the social class difference is minimal in that 8 per cent of these children are middle class, 7 per cent working class. While a total of 24 children received abstract explanations, 53 intervals of abstract speech are involved. So those children who received an abstract explanation are likely to receive more than one. Demands for 'Abstracts' from the children were very rare, these were asked by only 3 per cent of the children; one middle class child and four working class children. All these children were in the two oldest age groups.

Table 8.5 Instructions and demands for instructions to and from adults

Speech	Social Class	Mean No. of Intervals	F Ratio	Level of Significance
Instructions	MC	16		
			2.3	NS
	WC	13		
Demands for Instructions	MC	5		
			5.5	P<0.005
	WC	3		

	Family Position				Scheffé Comparison
Instructions	Eldest	13			
	Only	21	2.0	NS	
	Youngest	11			
Demands for Instructions	Eldest	3			O v. E P<0.05
	Only	9	6.2	P<0.003	O v. Y P<0.05
	Youngest	2			

(Scheffé comparisons omitted from the Table were non-significant)

E 'Options'

Eighty-four per cent of the children were offered 'Options' during the course of observation. Mothers were responsible for expressing the majority of the 'Options'. When 'Options' from all adults are combined or when maternal 'Options' only are considered, middle class adults are more likely to offer them than working class adults, but the difference is just not significant at the 0.01 level (see Table 8.6).

'Options' were also received from other children and middle class siblings were more likely to offer them than the working class siblings, Youngest children were most likely to be given them by older brothers and sisters. Fifty-three per cent of the children refused 'Options', i.e. said they specifically did not want to take part in what was suggested, or ignored the suggestion. This was more likely to happen among the middle class children, but the difference is not

Table 8.6   Options

Person Speaking	Social Class	Mean No. of Intervals	F Ratio	Level of Significance
Adult to Subject	MC	16	5.7	P<0.02
	WC	11		
Mother to Subject	MC	12	5.4	P<0.02
	WC	9		

significant at the 0.01 level (54 per cent of the middle class children; 46 per cent of the working class children, $\chi^2 = 4.4$; d.f. 1; P<0.04). Forty-seven per cent of the children asked or invited an adult to take part in an activity with them and were rejected or ignored by the adult and 84 per cent of the children asked for an 'Option' from an adult. Neither of these two measures varied with social class or any of the other independent variables.

F Affective speech

'Positive' speech was rarer then 'Negative' speech. Both types of speech varied with social class, the middle class children receiving more 'Positive' speech and less 'Negative' speech than the working class children. Neither varied with age or sex, but the incidence of 'Negative' speech tended to decline as the children grew older. 'Positive' speech showed a tendency to decline as the children grew older. 'Positive' speech showed a tendency to vary with family position, in that Eldest children were praised least, Only children most, while the 'Negative' speech varied significantly across family position. Eldest children were 'told off' most and Youngest children least. Maternal 'Positive' speech accounted for 74 per cent of all adult 'Positive' speech and 86 per cent of all adult 'Negative' speech (see Table 8.7)

Incidence of 'Positive' speech from the subjects to adults was rare, as it was between the subject and other children. Similarly 'Negative' speech from the children to the subject was too rare to make statistical analysis feasible, but aggressive speech from the

Table 8.7 'Positive' and 'Negative' speech

Speech	Social Class	Mean No. of Intervals	F Ratio	Level of Significance
Positive	MC	4		
	WC	2	8.7	P<0.01
Negative	MC	7		
	WC	16	16.3	P<0.001

	Family Position				Scheffé Comparison
Negative	Eldest	15			
	Only	12	6.1	P<0.01	E v. Y P<0.05
	Youngest	8			

child to other children occurred sufficiently consistently across the sample to permit analysis. While the subjects' aggressive speech did not differ according to social class, age or sex, Eldest children spoke more frequently in an aggressive way to other children than the other two groups (see Table 8.8).

Table 8.8 Aggressive speech to other children

Family Position	Mean No. of Intervals	F Ratio	Level of Significance
Eldest	8		
Only	5	4.4	P<0.01
Youngest	5		

G The relationship between speech and activities

It seemed likely that some activities were accompanied by more adult speech than others. To examine this relationship the proportion of time spent in an adult speech during specific activities was compared. General conversation was more likely to occur while the child was engaged in letter and number activities or being toileted or involved in a domestic activity than at any other time. Game playing 'Arrange and shape' activities and preparation for play activities were next likely to be accompanied by adult talk. Social dining, social physical games and clearing play activities follow. Given the steady decline in the proportion of time when adults did accompany other activities, no further calculations of the significance of these differences in the proportions have been made beyond play preparation compared to painting (see Table 8.9).

Table 8.9   Proportion of time spent in activities concurrent with adult speech to the subject

Activity	Proportion of Activity Accompanied by Adult Speech	Significance Levels Between Proportions
A Letter Activities	.80	A – D NS
B Number Activities	.77	
C Bathing, Toileting, Dressing	.75	
D Domestic; Cooking, Cleaning; Errand Running	.72	D – E P<.001
E Game Playing	.62	
F Arrange and Shape Activities	.62	
G Preparation for a 'Play' Activity	.59	E – G NS
H Social Dining	.57	F – H P<.001
I Social Physical Games	.56	G – I NS
J Clearing 'Play' Activities	.55	G – J P<.05
K Drawing	.53	G – K P<.005
L Painting	.51	G – L P<.001
M Ball Games	.50	
N Manipulation and Visual Object Exploration	.48	
O Animal Activities	.45	
P Watching people	.43	
Q Construction	.40	
R Higher Order Fantasy Play	.38	
All Other Activities	<.38	

(Being read to and being told a story are excluded as they are verbal activities by definition.)

In a similar manner, the relationship between particular activities and the proportion accompanying abstract and instructional speech was examined. In this analysis instructional and abstract speech items were combined. In terms of abstract and instructional speech, letter and number activities and looking at books differed significantly from each other and from all other forms of activity. Thus both letter and number activities were accompanied by high levels of general speech and instructional and abstract speech, but functional activities such as bathing, toileting and dressing gave rise more to general talk; they are not accompanied by 'Instructions' and 'Abstracts'. On the reverse, looking at books was relatively low in regard to general speech but what speech there was was highly informational. When the children were looking at books with an adult a great deal of the ensuing speech was in terms of naming and labelling objects in the pictures. 'Being read to' is excluded from this analysis because if the reading was interrupted by discussion of, for example, a word in the story or the accompanying pictures, the activity would no longer have been coded as 'Being read to' (see Table 8.10).

H Standford-Binet intelligence scores

Five of the children could not be given the Stanford-Binet Intelligence Test. Three of these children refused to participate and in two cases, administration was prevented by the children's illness and domestic family problems. Therefore, the data reported here are from the 160 children who participated in the test. Middle class children scored higher than working class children and boys scored higher than girls. While the mean for the Youngest children is lower than the other two family positions, the difference is not significant (see Table 8.11).

Discussion and conclusions

Social class differences are apparent on some of our speech measures but are not as widespread and striking as those found by, for example, Tough (1973) in a quasi-experimental setting. The number of speech intervals between the subjects and either adults

Table 8.10   Proportion of time spent in activities concurrent with instructional and abstract speech items from adults

Activity	Proportion of Activity Accompanied by Instructional and/or Abstract Speech	Significance Levels Between Proportions
A Letter Activities	.31	A – B P<0.001
B Number Activities	.25	B – C P<0.001
C Looking at Books	.17	C – D P<0.005
D Being Told a Story	.09	D – L NS
E Painting	.06	
F Arrange and Shape Activities	.06	
G Drawing	.05	
H Game Playing	.05	
I Manipulation and Visual Object Exploration	.02	
J Television Watching	.02	
K Domestic: Cooking, Clearing; Errand Running	.02	
L All Other Activities	.02	

or other children did not vary with social class. Similarly sex differences were not apparent, the girls were not interacting verbally more than the boys either generally with adults or specifically with their mothers. If this absence of difference was due to a lack of sensitivity in our measurement, it is difficult to see why family position affects were picked up so strikingly and consistently. Tizard *et al.* (1980) using a different measure from ours, 'hourly rate of conversations', in tape recorded speech in the home, similarly found no social class difference.

We do, however, find some social class differences in the qualitative speech measures designed to assess speech that would increase the child's vocabulary, classificatory ability and concept formation. Middle class adults are more likely, although the effect is just not significant at the 0.01 level, to provide their children with 'Instructions', but the children are significantly more likely to ask for 'Instructions'. It is possible that the quality of the 'Instructions' given

Table 8.11   Stanford-Binet IQ scores

Independent Variable		Mean	SD	F Ratio	Level of Significance
Social Class	MC	119	17	16.66	P<0.001
	WC	109	17		
Sex	m	111	16	8.35	P<0.005
	f	117	18		
Family Position	Eldest	115	19	1.55	NS
	Only	116	18		
	Youngest	110	13		

to the middle class children was different from that given to the working class children, a difference which our categorisation would not pick up. It might be that simple labelling 'Instructions' had been given more and that they had now reached a more advanced level and that this increased level of demands for 'Instructions' reflects this. This is not a postulate the data can answer quantitatively; anecdotal evidence taken from observers' notes would seem to confirm this. Incidents when parents provided their children with 'Instructions' which appeared to the observers to be redundant, since the child's previous conversation had shown he was well acquainted with these particular sets of labels such as common animals or parts of the body, seemed to be more prevalent among the working class group compared with the middle class group. Tizard *et al.* (1982) have made a detailed examination of 'cognitive demands' made to children in their own homes and at school. Cognitive demands required the child to use cognitive skills associated with labelling, identifying attributes (What colour is that one?), recalling, explaining and generalising and labelling in terms of the 3Rs. Rates of cognitive demands, either in hourly terms or as a proportion of general speech, did not vary between social classes. Working class children did, however, tend to receive more cognitive demands concerned with labelling and significantly more related to object attributes than the middle class children, i.e. the simpler cognitive demands.

We had anticipated a far greater number of abstract explanations among the middle class group than we actually encountered. After the study had begun and the infrequency of 'Abstracts' was noted, the observers were concerned that they were recording unreliably in this respect and 'missing' 'Abstracts'. Therefore, all speech which could possibly be defined as an 'Abstract' was noted down verbatim and discussed by all three observers. It became apparent that 'Abstracts' were genuinely very rare events. There appeared to be several interrelated reasons for this: an 'Abstract' explanation, as we defined it, is an extremely difficult thing to give to a young child. It takes considerable parental skill, thought and time. It is often simpler and more expedient when a busy parent is attempting to get through her domestic routine to answer cursorily, possibly in the form of an 'Instruction', than to take the time to think out an 'Abstract' reply.

Frequently a situation would arise where an 'Abstract' explanation would have been appropriate and the observer would wait with her pen poised, but the parent would hasten on, giving a brief reply and would not initiate the abstract explanation the situation begged. As mentioned in the Introduction, children of this age do not appear to have either the cognitive or linguistic maturity to follow up with a specific demand for an 'Abstract'. Tizard *et al.* (1983) attempted to subdivide 'Why' questions in their tape recordings of children's speech at home. They found questions with 'a strong claim to be considered as expressions of intellectual puzzlement' rare but came across conversations between children and their mothers when the children asked a series of related questions which successively led to an elaborated explanation. This type of sequence of questions and answers was not included in our 'Abstract' and 'Demand for Abstract' categories. These had been designed, in part, to tap the actual occurrence in the home of the type of questions posed to mothers by Bernstein's colleagues (Bernstein, 1972), and reported to yield very different answers, dependent on the mother's social class. This study and the findings of Tizard *et al.* would suggest that parents of preschool children rarely have to respond, in a natural situation, to demands from their preschool children for an expanded explanation, expressed in a single, complete, question.

'Options' and adult 'Positive' and 'Negative' speech showed consistent social class differences. 'Options' are a potent tool for controlling the child's behaviour so that it conforms to the parents' wishes. They were used to distract the child when he was about to engage in something the parents considered socially undesirable and so to prevent a *'contretemps'*, but also in less immediate situations: for instance, when a child became bored and restive, a tactful 'Option' would direct his attention to a new and involving activity and preclude potential irritability. This may explain in part the lower rates of middle class adult 'Negative' speech, in that situations which demand adult verbal punishment did not so often arise or continue. However, the increased middle class 'Positive' speech rates suggest that to some extent there was a social class dichotomy along the 'carrot and stick' line, also found by Lytton (1979) and Lytton and Zwirner (1975). In some families there were very high rates of either 'Positive' or 'Negative' speech; in these cases it is feasible that, although every effort was made to prevent this, the observers' criteria shifted and it is possible that these group differences are underestimated. That the middle class children were also receiving more 'Options' from their peers, suggests that it is a highly imitative form of communication and that older siblings were developing similar tactics to their parents towards their siblings.

Family position differences exist and are consistent over a number of language measures. They match the differences found in social interaction, but it must be borne in mind that to some extent these measures overlap, as social participation was based in part on verbal communication. It can therefore be argued that the family position effects found with language are attributable to the same causes outlined for social participation in Chapter 5. Only and Eldest children were receiving more adult verbal attention than Youngest children, with Only children receiving most except in the case of adult 'Negative' speech, where Eldest exceeded Only children. Probably this was attributable to the additional adult 'Negative' speech arising from sibling disputes, while parents, generally, displayed a 'laissez-faire' approach to the Youngest children in contrast to Eldest and Only children. Again, mirroring the pattern found with social participation, Youngest children were engaging in most child/child speech.

From our analysis of auto-talk, it is apparent that children who displayed frequent social talk did not also engage in high levels of auto-talk: on the contrary, auto-talk occurred when children had less opportunity for social speech from both adults and other children. When both adult and child speech were taken into account, the amount of 'talking to' and 'being talked to' was the same for each of the three family position groups and this accounts for the lack of difference in amounts of auto-talk between them.

The significant differences between the proportions of time spent in adult speech accompanying activities suggest that some activities are particularly conducive to general conversation, instructional and abstract explanations, or both. Both toiletry activities and domestic activities prompted high levels of general speech, but not of instructional or abstract explanations. Conversation was often geared to the task in hand, but also these activities provided occasions for general conversation about family and domestic affairs. Game playing was a social activity by definition and therefore depended on some verbal communications, while 'Arrange and shape' activities frequently led to discussions on which piece belonged where. Letter, number and 'Looking at book' activities stand out, in that order as particularly likely to be accompanied by instruction and abstract explanations.

Letter and number activities with children of the sample age are essentially verbal and totally dependent on guidance from an adult or older child. While a few of the children were acquainted with some letter names, the majority were not. More children were familiar with single digit number names. Many of the number activities in which the children engaged involved simple counting. At this level the children were probably better informed numerically than with the comparative letter naming activities. Counting occurs naturally in adult speech in a way that letter naming does not: for example, counting before lifting a child over an obstacle, 'One, two, three, up!'; or counting to hurry a child, 'Now get all those toys away before I count to ten: one, two ...'. Thus there was less need for continuous instruction in number activities than was required in letter activities. When looking at books, the adult/child conversation usually consisted of naming and labelling the picture and explaining what was happening.

Girls neither spoke nor received more general or particular forms of speech. As suggested in the Introduction, it may be that our measures are not subtle enough to pick up any sex differences existing in the sample's age range, but as the data stand, there is no evidence of female advantage or maternal inclination to favour daughter's speech. One sex difference was apparent, the girls were more inclined to sing or hum than the boys. Singing with either parent was so rare that a statistical analysis was impossible. Intuitively, singing Nursery Rhymes and childish songs does appear to be a feminine activity.

However, significant sex and social class differences are apparent in the Standford-Binet Intelligence Test scores. The majority of Stanford-Binet items have a verbal content. In an attempt to examine whether the score differences were essentially linguistically based, items were classified as either involving verbal comprehension alone, or dependent for success on both verbal comprehension and expressed speech. We argued that if linguistic factors were potent in accounting for the middle class children and the girls having higher scores than the working class children and boys, the difference on items where both verbal comprehension and expressed speech were essential should be significantly greater than when the other items were compared. But this was not the case. Arguably, this may be because the differences are not linguistically based, or this was not a valid division of the test items in terms of assessing verbal skills.

The higher scores of the middle class children can be attributed in part to their greater experience of activities similar to those demanded by the Stanford-Binet Intelligence Test. Many of the items depend on matching or describing pictures and the middle class children had more experience of books. Also items are similar to those encountered in children's 'Arrange and shape' games and activities with which the middle class children had more experience. In addition, a problem which the test administrators encountered with a few of the subjects was that of getting the child to wait long enough to hear the entire verbal instruction before starting on a test item, which accords with the 'reflection – impulsiveness' dimensions described by Kagan (1966). This type of response style was particularly noticeable in a small number of working class children whose Stanford-Binet IQ scores were exceptionally low, but whose social skills and powers of observation had been noticeably adroit during observation sessions. For example, one 3½-year-old working class girl scored in the 80s but was capable of competently washing up the family's dishes after a meal entirely on her own. The observer also witnessed the following incident. It was an early morning observation, the child had just woken up and was sitting in an armchair beside the fire, in her pyjamas, dozing. Her father was collecting his things for work. Her mother was getting breakfast in the kitchen. Her father

inspected a packet of cigarettes and found it was empty, surreptiti-
ously looked at his daughter, sneaked three of the remaining few
cigarettes out of a packet of his wife's cigarettes lying on a table next
to the child, stuffed them in his haversack and left the house. Half
an hour later, her mother opened her packet of cigarettes and
exclaimed 'Where've all my fags gone?' The child giggled 'Dad
nicked three of 'em before he went'.

None of these arguments accounting for the superior test performance by the middle class children can be used to account for the
female superior performance. If the girls were more cognitively and
verbally advanced than the boys, it is not reflected in their activities
or speech. One other possible variable to account for this difference
is the sex of the tester, which in all cases was female. It is feasible
that the girls were finding it easier to relate to the female administrators and thus produced enhanced scores compared with the boys.

In the Introduction it was made clear that Bernstein's work had
influenced the speech categories we used and led us to make some
specific predictions. The middle class parents' enhanced use of 'Options' and 'Positive' speech fits in with the Bernsteinian distinction between the imperative mode of control and the mode based upon
appeals. A finer examination of the speech we globally recorded on
 Negative' adult speech would repay investigation. However, at variance with Bernstein's theory is the remarkable lack of 'Abstract'
explanations offered by adults to middle class children. It does seem
likely that when adults or children are asked to take part in experiments in laboratory settings, or under quasi-natural conditions
(Tough, 1973) linguistic social class differences are enhanced to an
extent which makes generalisations referring to the home setting
invalid.

Chapter 9
Attendance at, and attitude to, preschool provision

Six different types of preschool provision were available in the sample area: Toddlers' Clubs, Play Groups, Nursery Schools, Nursery Classes, Reception Classes (where children were accepted under the age of five years) and Day Nurseries. Availability to individual families varied considerably across the sample area and, as will be shown, availability cannot be considered only on a geographical basis. In the interview we asked parents what types of preschool provision the children had attended, were attending, and would be attending in the future. As the children who were already at Nursery School or attending Play Group for over two sessions a week had been deliberately excluded from the sample, we are not examining a representative sample of children from the area as a whole, in terms of their preschool attendance. Where possible, figures including all the children contacted are given. We also wished to find out why parents were using one type of facility over another and what advantages and disadvantages they saw in the main types of preschool facilities. In the pilot study, we found that parents made no distinction between Nursery Schools and Classes, so we therefore asked parents for their opinions about the two most prevalent forms of preschool provision, Play Groups and Nursery Schools and Classes as a combined category.

A Current attendance at Toddlers' Clubs

Only 6 children were still attending Toddlers' Clubs. One of these children was working class and four were middle class. In addition, one middle class child went to both Toddlers' Club and Play Group one session per week each. A few children were rejected from the sample because Toddlers' Club attendance was included with Play Group attendance to give them a total of 3 or more sessions of attendance per week.

B Current attendance at Play Group

Fifty-three per cent of the sample were attending Play Group at the time of initial contact. The mean starting age was 2.8 years and did not vary with the child's social class background, sex or family position. The majority of children who did attend, went for two sessions a week. Of the 1,183 children contacted in the study, 5 per cent were rejected from the final sample because they attended Play Group for three or more sessions a week. Although it is not possible to reliably give a social class break down for these children, they tended to live in the more expensive housing areas and were therefore probably from middle class families.

Table 9.1   Play Group attendance expressed in percentages according to social class

Play Group Attendance	Middle Class	Working Class
Attending one session per week	12	8
Attending two sessions per week	57	29
Attending sometimes (Play Bus)	1	1
Had discontinued attendance	11	10
Parents proposed future attendance	4	9
No past, current or proposed attendance	30	43

(χ^2 comparison of the number of middle class and working class children attending Play Group, i.e. first three groups combined: $\chi^2 = 13.4$; d.f. 1; P<0.001)

Reasons why an appreciable number of the children had discontinued going to Play Group (see Table 9.1) were varied. Two of the middle class children had suffered serious illness and, although they were fully recovered at the time of the study, their parents seemed to have 'got out of the habit' of taking them. In two working class families practical difficulties had intervened: one family had moved to an area where no group was available, and in the other the birth of a baby made it impossible for the mother to continue taking the older child. The remaining children had only attended for one or two sessions before stopping. With a couple of the children, mothers felt they were not yet ready for the Play Group, the child having seemed too young to cope with the situation. Similarly, two other children had screamed and cried when first taken and the parents had concluded the child did not like going and so they did not wish to persist. A few parents had actively disliked the supervisor and other parents they had met there, which had discouraged them from continuing to take their child. This seemed to occur where a Play Group drew children from both private and council estates, the council tenants feeling that the private house-owning parents were 'snobbish' and despised them. Other mothers produced idiosyncratic reasons for not going any more: that the attendant mothers were a bad influence on the children; that there was too much free play and this would make settling down at school difficult. Finally, one mother had deliberately taken her child for one session because she had been curious to see 'What went on at Play Group.'

Probably the majority of parents who said they proposed sending their children to Play Group were not being realistic and this may be because in the circumstances it may have appeared to them as a socially desirable answer. Several of the children were already over three-and-a-half years of age and one was over four years. There is no difference in the number of boys and girls who were attending Play Group or where they came in the family. However, there is a highly significant class difference in that middle class children were much more likely to be attending than working class children.

C Nursery School, Class and Infant School attendance

As parents in our interview were very uncertain of distinctions between Nursery Schools, Nursery Classes and Infant Schools, information on children contacted and rejected because they were attending any of the three has been treated together. As in the Play

Group analysis, no social class breakdown is possible for these children, who made up 37 per cent of all the children contacted (N = 1,183).

In the interview, parents were asked if they expected their children to attend Nursery School or Nursery Class, and at what age they anticipated their children would go. If the parents were able to give the name of the school this was recorded and checked to see if it was a Nursery School or if a Nursery Class existed. Parents proved very unreliable in distinguishing between Nursery Schools, Nursery Classes, and the Reception Classes in Infants' Schools. There were no significant differences in terms of the parents' social class, the child's sex or his position in the family for the ages given by the parents, so the results are presented for the sample as a whole (see Table 9.2).

Table 9.2   Age parents gave for commencing Nursery School or Class

Nursery School and Nursery Class Attendance		Percentage of Sample
No attendance anticipated		52
Anticipated Age of Attendance	3–3½ years	9
	3½–4 years	20
	4–4½ years	10
	4½–5 years	5
Attendance discontinued		1
Not known if child would attend		3

According to the parents, the children were most frequently entering Nursery School or Class aged between three-and-a-half and four years; slightly fewer children were first attending between three and three-and-a-half years, and four and four-and-a-half years. A small group of children were going when they were over four-and-a-half years, which, if the parents were correct, would probably have been to Nursery Classes. A further 10 per cent of the children were going to go to Infant Schools before they were four-and-a-half years. Nineteen per cent of the children were going to go to Infant School after they had become five, having had no previous Nursery or School experience. Most of these children came from two specific school catchment areas and the parents vociferously pointed out the unfairness when their situation was compared with surrounding areas.

D Day Nurseries

Only one child in the sample was known to have attended a Day Nursery for a period before the time of the study.

E Reasons parents gave for sending or not sending their children to Play Group or Nursery School or Class

In our introduction aimed at enlisting parents' co-operation, we explained that one reason we were doing the study was to compare the benefits of children's experience at home with those at Nursery School. In addition, we had just asked parents the questions about current or anticipated attendance of Play Group and Nursery School. This undoubtedly alerted parents to some extent to the existence of these facilities. We deliberately chose to use an open question to elicit reasons for their proposed actions, as we did not wish to lead parents into invalidly choosing between previously prepared statements. Parents were asked either why their child was going or would go to Play Group, or why he was not going to Play Group and similar questions for Nursery School attendance. Inevitably, this produced a very wide range of answers; some parents gave only one reason, others several. One disadvantage of this form of questioning was that we suspected that a number of parents were not prepared to admit to the interviewer that they were unaware of the existence of one or other of the facilities.

Broadly, the reasons given could be grouped under five main headings:

1 Reasons concerned with the social, educational and emotional development of the child.
2 Reasons based on the attributes of the facilities.
3 The child was sent on the suggestion or advice of someone.
4 Practical reasons dictated whether the child attended or not.
5 The parents specifically said that they did not know of the facility or had not considered it.

Reasons given did not vary with the sex of the child or position in the family, but did show significant class differences in some respects. The data are therefore presented separately, according to social class. Reasons why children had discontinued Play Group seemed distinct from reasons why children were not going to attend Play Group at all and have been mentioned previously. The data here are based on the 148 children who had never discontinued Play Group attendance and the percentages in the tables are expressed in terms of the proportion of parents giving that reason within each social class.

1 Reasons centred on the child's development

This type of reason was by far the most frequently given in favour of both Play Group and Nursery School attendance, by both social classes; although significantly more middle class parents gave 'developmental' reasons for wanting their children to attend Play Group than did working class parents ($X^2 = 15.02$; d.f. 1; P<0.005).

Parents' most frequently voiced reason for sending their child to either Play Group or Nursery School was so that he could mix with other children. Middle class parents particularly saw this as an attribute of Play Groups. Parents saw both facilities as a preparation for the child for the next 'stage' of his preschool or school career.

Both facilities were considered educational, Nursery Schools only slightly more than Play Groups. Children were seen by some parents as bored at home and they felt that the stimulation of Play Group and Nursery School could alleviate this. Some parents thought that either or both facilities would provide discipline for the children, making them more independent and giving them confidence. A couple of parents gave the nebulous reply that the child was 'ready to go', and one working class mother simply sent her child to Play Group because she thought he would enjoy it (see Table 9.3).

Middle class mothers seemed more in favour of keeping their children at home than working class mothers, especially where Nursery School was concerned. This is included as a child-centred reason. A small percentage of parents thought children nowadays had quite enough school experience without adding to it at the younger end of the scale. A few middle class mothers were so content with the children's Play Group experience that they were therefore not wanting to send their children on to Nursery School. That the child was ready for the next stage of his preschool or initial school career seemed to some parents a reason for not sending their children to an earlier facility (see Table 9.4).

Table 9.3   Reasons in favour of the child going to Play Group or Nursery School

Reasons	Play Group		Nursery School	
	MC	WC	MC	WC
To mix with other children	69	40	19	40
A preparation for Nursery/Infant School	15	8	16	20
Seen as educational	7	8	13	12
To give independence/discipline/confidence	13	5	7	4
Child bored at home	4	6	7	7
Child ready to go	3	–	3	–
Mother thought the child would enjoy it	–	1	–	–

Table 9.4   Reasons against sending child to Play Group or Nursery School

Reasons	Play Group		Nursery School	
	MC	WC	MC	WC
Prefer child at home	5	5	16	5
Children are long enough at school without extra preschool years	–	–	5	5
Child happy at Play Group, does not wish to transfer him to Nursery School	–	–	5	–
Ready for Nursery School or Infant School	5	–	3	1

2 Reasons centred on the attributes of the two facilities

Both types of provision were seen by a small number of parents from both social classes to provide more equipment and facilities for the children than could be achieved at home (see Table 9.5).

Table 9.5   Reason for sending the child to Play Group or Nursery School

Reason	Play Group		Nursery School	
	MC	WC	MC	WC
More equipment and facilities than at home	3	3	3	5

An appreciable number of middle class mothers thought that Nursery School hours were too long for children of preschool age. In the Stoke-on-Trent area, Nursery Schools tend to take children full-time as opposed to part-time and so these mothers were probably thinking in terms of a full day. A few people gave an unqualified comment that they just did not approve of a particular type of facility. A few middles class mother thought that there was too much free play at both Play Group and Nursery School and felt that this was a definite disadvantage. A couple of mother thought Play Group hours were too brief; also that mothers' attendance at Play Group was a disadvantage. Individual mothers objected to Play Group staff being untrained and the age range of the children attending being too broad (see Table 9.6).

3 The child attended following suggestions and advice

Only a small number of parents were sending their children to Nursery School on advice or at someone's suggestion. Included in this group are parents who said they had not thought why their children were going to go: 'Well, they all do round here.' The professional advice was given by a Health Visitor in all cases; a few parents had accepted the suggestion of a friend (see Table 9.7)

Table 9.6   Reasons against both or either facility

Reasons	Play Group		Nursery School	
	MC	WC	MC	WC
Too many hours involved	–	–	9	1
General disapproval	1	3	1	1
Too much free play	5	–	4	–
Too few hours involved	1	1	–	–
Mothers are a bad influence in Play Group	1	1	–	–
Staff are untrained	–	1	–	–
The age range is too great	1	–	–	–

Table 9.7   Attendance following suggestions or advice

Reasons	Play Group		Nursery School	
	MC	WC	MC	WC
Social convention	–	–	1	2
Professional advice	–	1	–	2
Suggestion from a friend	–	2	–	1

4 Practical reasons dictating the child's attendance at Play Group or Nursery School

A few parents were wanting their children to attend because it suited themselves. Usually mothers voiced it as 'to give me a break' so that they had some time when they could go shopping or get on with jobs at home unimpeded by the demands of their child (see Table 9.8). Practicalities were most frequently voiced as the reason against children's Nursery School or Play Group attendance. There is no significant difference between classes for negative practical reasons concerning Nursery School, but the practical reasons for not sending children to Play Group show a significant class difference ($\chi^2 = 7.18$; d.f. 1; P<0.01).

Table 9.8   Practical reason in favour of attendance

	Play Group		Nursery School	
Reason	MC	WC	MC	WC
Parental convenience	7	3	1	6

More working class parents reported that Play Groups were unavailable or that it was unfeasible to take their children there. Some parents had been assured of a place shortly, either at Nursery School or Infant School, and therefore considered it impractical to start the children at Play Group, or at Nursery School if Infant School was in question. A few middle class mothers had their children down for Nursery School but were convinced that the length of the waiting list made their children's actual attendance unlikely. Only one parent, a working class mother, did not send her child to Play Group because of the expense; she had two eligibly aged preschool children and her husband was out of work.

Table 9.9   Practical reasons against sending children to Play Group or Nursery School

	Play Group		Nursery School	
Reasons	MC	WC	MC	WC
Unavailable	6	15	16	17
Unfeasible	3	9	1	6
Attendance at Nursery School or Infant School definitely arranged and about to commence	–	3	4	2
Waiting list too long	–	–	4	–
Too expensive	–	1	–	–

5 Play Group or Nursery School were not known to parents

A few parents did specifically say they had not heard of either Nursery School or Play Group; in addition some said they had not considered sending their children, or gave the reply 'I'm not bothered' in such a way that the interviewers were convinced that at the most the parents knew very little about the facility. Knowledge of facilities did vary significantly between social classes. Middle class parents knew less about Nursery Schools, while working class parents knew less about Play Groups ($x^2 = 8.86$; d.f. 1; P<0.01) (see Table 9.10).

Table 9.10   Ignorance of facilities

Reason	Play Group		Nursery School	
	MC	WC	MC	WC
Did not know of facility	–	8	6	–
Had not considered facility	–	3	3	1

Discussion and conclusions

The high proportion of children in the sample attending Play Group and anticipating attending Nursery School or Class reflect the figures in the area and compare very favourably with those at a national level as, for instance, estimated by Hughes *et al.* (1980) as 18.5 per cent for Play Group attendance and 15 per cent for Nursery School or Nursery Class places. However, the Play Group attendance does show a definite class bias. While there have been a number of attempts to set up Play Groups specifically in deprived areas, notably by the Save the Children Fund, the general consensus in the literature is that Play Groups are essentially organised by, and serve, a middle class clientele. McCreesh and Maher (1976) in their brief history of the Preschool Play Groups Association, describe the parents involved as 'largely middle class'. Van der Eyken (1977) reviews a number of small locally based surveys which similarly conclude that Play Groups are typically middle class because the organsiation and potential financial back up are beyond the scope of most working class women. Van der Eyken also considers that the commitment and ability to transport children for relatively short periods in the day are also going to dissuade working class mothers from taking their children. This seems to be true for this sample. Availability of Play Groups seems to be a matter of parental perception, although an important practical factor is that far fewer working class mothers have access to a car to transport their children. Thus an essentially similar effort may make Play Group attendance unavailable or unfeasible to one group and not to another.

Ignorance of what is available for their children also appears important in contributing to parents' non-use of facilities. Our study shows a surprising difference between classes in this respect, the working class mothers being less informed about Play Groups but not about Nursery Schools. All groups were ill informed about distinctions between Nursery School, Class and Infant Schools. Earlier studies in other parts of the country have also shown that many parents are unaware of the available facilities; for example Moss, Tizard and Crook's (1973) surveys near Liverpool and in London, and the East Newcastle Action Group Survey (1971) in that area. In the present study we found it necessary to explain the difference between Play Groups and Nursery Schools to a few Health Visitors, who were involved in contacting potential sample children. In a later study we have encountered two head teachers of Infant Schools who had never heard of Play Groups. The lack of information therefore seems widespread. Discussing this problem with some Nottingham Nursery teachers, they said they were well aware of it but felt that if they 'advertised' their schools this would unfairly raise parents' hopes, as they already had more children on their waiting lists than they could accommodate. However, if demand does exceed the number of available places, selection in terms of better informed parents hardly seems justified. This ignorance may explain the absence of differences in our sample in terms of present or projected attendance according to sex or family position. People were sending their children if they knew about the facilities rather than making informed decisions where these factors might have weight.

Since only parents who had sent their children to Play Groups said they disapproved of a specific local group, this does suggest that those who had discontinued sending their children for this reason had genuinely encountered snobbery or some feeling of personal exclusion. The Preschool Play Groups Association would of course be strongly opposed to any attempts by a group to make themselves appear exclusive. However, the Play Groups depend on the responsibility, energy and initiative of local people, which in many ways are their strength, and personality problems are bound to occur. As mentioned earlier, where private and council housing areas abut and the council tenants are probably in the minority, there is potential for this type of problem. We also felt that if parents had been better forewarned that children are often very tearful when first going to Play Group, but that with a little persistence they will enjoy and benefit from the experience, parents would not have been put off after only one or two sessions.

It does seem essential that an effort is made to inform both the public and professions in closely allied fields about what preschool facilities do exist and what these facilities offer children. Health Visitors are in a prime position to act in this capacity and a few of our children were attending Play Group on a Health Visitor's advice; similarly, primary school teachers have opportunity to advise parents who have older children at their school or when parents call to put their children's names down for the school. Local Play Groups sometimes put up posters at their local clinic and perhaps Nursery Schools and Classes could also do this and Nursery Schools, Classes and Intant Schools could display Play Group posters. Information could also be displayed or pamphlets made available at antenatal clinics and maternity hospitals. Most parents of preschool children have to visit commercial places such as Mothercare or Boots' Baby Counter; possibly such firms could be asked to co-operate. Secondary schools might include this information briefly in Civics courses.

Chapter 10
A comparison of home and preschool

In the preceding chapters we have described the young child's life and experiences at home. We will now attempt a comparison between the child's home experiences and his experiences at Nursery School, Nursery Class, Play Group and Day Nursery, the four types of preschool facility studied by Hutt *et al.* in the sister research project conducted at Keele: 'Play, Exploration and Learning'.

There are problems in making valid comparisons. Observations in the four preschool contexts were made in 'Free Play' periods. There are no equivalent periods in the home, where the child's activities do not occur at set times and his schedule fits in with his own family's affairs, which is why the Home Study sampled an entire waking day in the child's home life. Thus, the Home study includes, for instance, the time the child spent in toiletry activities and meal times. Therefore a straight comparison of percentage time spend in different activites would minimise the time the Home child spent in activities similar to those engaged in at 'Free Play' periods at the four preschool facilities. To correct for this, Table 10.1 compares the time spent in the home in activities equivalent to those engaged in at preschool, and in addition includes domestic activities found only in the home and two activities with materials which were not seen, and therefore not categorised, at preschool, namely 'Packing' and 'String play'.

Superficially, two factors influence the child's choice of activity: availability of that activity and the child's own idiosyncratic preferences for particular activities. The picture is not so clear cut. Whereas a piece of apparatus essential to some activity may not be physically present, the child's perceptions of its availability will also influence whether he chooses to use it or not, and social factors may mediate in the child's choice of physically available equipment and objects, as Tizard *et al.,* (1976) have suggested.

Table 10.1 Comparison of percentage of time spent in different forms of activity at home and at Nursery School, Nursery Class, Play Group and Day Nursery

Activities	H	NS	NC	PG	DN
Sand Play	1	5	6	5	<1
Water Play	3	2	10	4	4
Soft Modelling/Clay	1	3	6	2	1
Painting	1	2	3	4	6
Colouring and Drawing	3	2	<1	<1	1
Collage Type Activities	1	5	2	5	3
Construction	3	6	6	6	9
Packing	1	–	–	–	–
String Play	1	–	–	–	–
Arrange & Shape/Puzzles	3	4	2	2	1
Records, Radio, Noise/Music	1	2	<1	<1	2
Television	12	<1	0	0	<1
Books	7	5	3	2	5
Physical Activity	27	15	17	23	16
Tactile/Visual Object Manipulation	3	2	1	3	3
Dressing-Up	1	1	9	8	4
Representational Fantasy Play	11	4	9	8	4
Fantasy Object Play	1	3	8	4	4
Fantasy Person Play	1	4	3	2	6
Immaterial Fantasy Play	1	2	4	1	2
Specific & General Looking/Watching	13	27	20	28	26
Animal Activities	1	–	–	–	–
Cooking	1	–	–	–	–
General Household and Garden Maintenance	1	–	–	–	–
Running Errands	1	–	–	–	–

In the course of the sister project, family grouping was introduced into three of the six Day Nurseries used in the study. This had the effect of making some equipment physically unavailable to some of the Day Nursery children. This probably accounts for less time being spent in particular activities in the Day Nurseries compared with the other preschool contexts. It is, for instance, impractical to have a sand trough out and accessible to younger members of the family group who may well consume the sand. The dressing up box and Wendy House were not available to children based in rooms where these items were not present. Similarly, although children were free to travel to different parts of the Nursery School, if the dressing up clothes and the Wendy House were not located in the child's 'own' classroom, it called for a special expedition for the child to go and take part in dressing up or representational fantasy play in the Wendy House. These two items were more easily available to children in Nursery Classes or Play Groups where the facility was normally confined to one room.

In the home, sand play, as we have described, was usually opportune, in that it often took place with granulated materials such as sugar, biscuit crumbs and soil at the edges of gardens. Clay, plasticine and other commercially produced children's modelling materials were infrequently encountered. Incidents when children took part in cooking and had access to pastry or dough were very rare. Hutt *et al.* report that clay activities appealed more to older children and the mean age of the children in the sample attending Nursery Class is highest and this is where the children were spending most time in activities with clay. Although 73 per cent of the Home children had access to painting material, occasions of painting activity were more likely among the middle class children, and, as we have already pointed out, preparing for a painting session in the home requires considerable adult time and supervision. In contrast, colouring and drawing materials were readily available in the home, are easily available and relatively 'unmessy' and were used more in the home than in the preschool contexts. Activities which could be compared with the full-scale collage work engaged in particularly at Nursery Schools and Play Groups were virtually not observed at all in the home. It is very understandable that parents are disinclined to encourage their children to participate in the messier types of play with materials when often space is limited and the only area where they can take place is carpeted.

Specific number activities occurred very rarely in the preschool settings and so were recorded in the puzzle category. For comparability, the small percentage of time children spent in number activities has been included in 'Arrange and shape puzzles'. Home children were spending an approximately similar amount of time in this type of activity as children in the preschool contexts. Little time was spent listening to the radio or records and in noise-making in the home as was so in the preschool contexts. While television watching hardly occurred in the latter, it occupies a considerable amount of the child's time at home.

Specific letter activities, like number activities, were rarely seen in the preschool contexts and were included in activities with books. Therefore, comparing all book activities, that is both looking at books or any printed material and being read to across all contexts, Home children spent slightly more time in this type of activity than did the children in any of the preschool contexts.

Hutt *et al.* point out that the high level of physical activity in the Play Groups is attributable to the free access which children have to physical equipment, whereas this tends to be restricted to outdoor play time in the other facilities. To some extent this is true in the home; where a child, as with the majority of children, had a vehicle type toy it was generally available, but so also was the furniture which provided the equipment for the climbing, swinging and bouncing. In addition, some of the physical activity engaged in at home would not have been permitted in the preschool contexts, while ball play which occurred frequently in the home is a rare preschool activity.

Wendy House play accounts for a considerable proportion of representational fantasy play in the preschool context. As we have pointed out, this is less available to Nursery School and Day Nursery children and probably accounts for the shorter periods of time spent in representational fantasy play at these two facilities. In the home, there is the stimulation of 'real' objects which can be used in representational fantasy play, as opposed to toy replica objects. This may contribute to the higher incidence of representational fantasy play in the home. At home, it is possible for a child to spend long periods in essentially repetitive representational fantasy play, such as parking and reparking long lines of miniature cars, or setting out and resetting out dolls' tea sets and miniature saucepans. In the preschool context, this type of activity is difficult to pursue without interference from other children. In an analysis of the Home data, we showed that adult participation increased fantasy play, while child participation had no effect in increasing or decreasing it. Incidence of fantasy object, fantasy person and immaterial fantasy play is greater in the preschool contexts compared with home. This higher incidence does not seem to be attributable to adult involvement in fantasy activities in the preschool settings. Hutt *et al.* report that only two out of four hundred and thirty-five overtures from children to adults were concerned with fantasy and in neither of these cases was the staff response conducive to extending the fantasy play. It is therefore possible that child participation in fantasy play operates in a different way at home and at preschool, and that participation in representational fantasy play by other children facilitates the emergence of the other three categories of fantasy play.

The children at home spent far less time looking about and watching other people and activities surrounding them than the children in all the preschool contexts. Inevitably there will be a great deal more activity to watch, compared with the activities of the limited number of individuals at home. It is possible that, in part, the increased looking and watching at preschool may also reflect a lack of ease on the part of the children. Hutt *et al.* found that unspecific looking about decreased as the child settled into Nursery School.

In presenting data which was comparative across the home and preschool contexts we pointed out the problem of comparing 'Free Play' periods in the preschool context with the entire waking day of the Home child. The same problem exists when examining the amount of time children spend in joint activities with adults and other children. Therefore, we have made this comparison only in terms of the activities listed in Table 10.1. In addition, in the home the child usually interacted with an adult on a one-to-one basis. This is not the case in the preschool context. In Figure 10.1. we therefore present the overall time spent in joint activities with adults and also indicate that proportion of joint time with adults in the different preschool contexts which might take place on an individual basis. This was calculated by dividing the overall joint adult/child time by the observed adult/child ratios, obtained by means of scan sampling by Hutt *et al.* in each preschool context.

The children at home spent less time in overall joint activities with adults than the children at Nursery Schools and Play Groups, but more time than those at Nursery Classes and Day Nurseries. The mean time a child spent in joint activities with an adult at home on

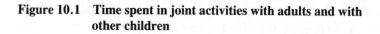

Figure 10.1   Time spent in joint activities with adults and with other children

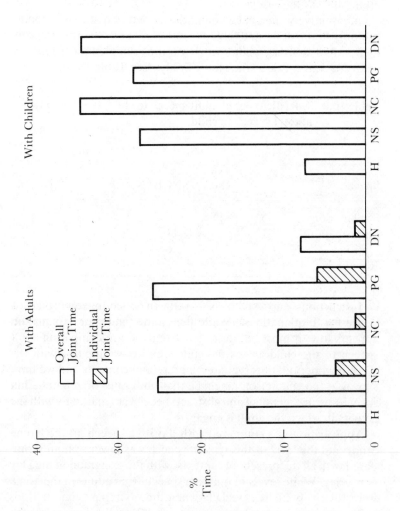

a one to to one basis probably far exceeds all the preschool contexts, which is an inevitable consequence of preschool child/staff ratios. Predictably, in all the preschool contexts a much greater proportion of the child's time was spent in joint activities with other children than was the case at home.

Quantitatively, language comparisons between the two studies can only be made tentatively, as Hutt *et al.* used the utterance as their unit of analysis, while speech was time sampled according to a one-zero convention in the Home Study. (see Table 10.2)

Table 10.2   Specific types of adult speech to child as a percentage of total speech to child

Speech	Home	NS Teacher	NNEB	NC NNEB	PG	DN NNEB
Explanations	5	13	10	9	8	4
Approbation	1	6	11	6	3	1
Option	4	6	6	1	3	1
Rebuke	5	3	2	0	1	9

'Instructions' and 'Abstracts' have been added together to give a figure for 'Explanations'. While the Home figure for explanation appears low, it must be borne mind that we are comparing adult speech to the child across the child's entire waking day with the 'Free play period' observed in the preschool contexts and we have shown in the chapter on language that both rates of general adult speech and instructional and abstract speech vary markedly with the activity in which the child is engaged.

Approbation was compared with 'Positive speech' in the Home Study and the level of this type of speech was lower at home compared with all the preschool contexts, with the exception of the Day Nurseries. While levels of optional speech from adults in the home were relatively high, especially when the discrepant time periods being compared are taken into account, 'Negative speech' in the Home Study was equated with 'Rebuke' and here children were being reproved more in the home than any of the preschool contexts, with the exception of the Day Nurseries.

In a direct comparison of the speech of children at home and at Nursery School, Tizard *et al.* (1980) found that adult/child conversations at home were more frequent, longer and more evenly balanced between the adult and the child than at Nursery School. They also found that, whereas speech differences between social classes were minimal at home, the gap widened at school. At school, working class children were more likely to approach a teacher for help in disputes than middle class children, but middle class children asked more questions and gave information to teachers more often, took part in more teacher/child conversations, spoke for longer to the teachers and maintained these conversations more. They conclude that these findings support the observers' impressions that the working class children were 'less confident' at Nursery School than the middle class children.

Bryant, Harris and Newton (1980) in their study of children with their parents and with their child minders concluded that the children were inhibited, passive and 'too' quiet at the child minders'. While the latter authors' study includes children of a much younger age than would be attending Nursery School, it seems likely that young children will be less at ease in situations away from their own home and parents. Our evidence that children spend far more time in preschool contexts watching other people and looking about than do those at home, supports this conclusion. To some extent the higher levels of 'Rebukes' received by children in the home also reflect this; children were more likely to provoke a situation by doing something of which they knew their parents disapproved than those in equivalent situations in the preschool contexts: in other words, children were on their 'best behaviour' away from home. Similarly, parents did not make the relatively superfical approbation frequently made by Nursery Staff, such as quoted by Hutt *et al.*: 'Oh, beautiful. Make him a bit fatter', which explains why lower levels of positive speech were recorded in the home.

Although there was a very small group of children in the Home sample who received very little verbal stimulation and encouragement from their parents, this was certainly not true for the majority of children from both social classes. In the case of one exceptional working class child, almost every verbal overture he made to his parents was received in silence or with a monosyllable. Two other children, both working class, took part in very little general conversation with adults and received exceptionally high levels of adult negative speech. While conversation between adults and children was often disjointed and showed rapid subject changes, parents would often pause in what they were doing or when actively engaged with the child and pursue a point that interested the child.

In the Home Study we made a number of tape recordings for checking reliabilities of the speech coding. The following is a typical example of a recording of a mother/daughter (3 years, 2 months) pair. The child is sitting on her mother's lap having just had lunch. The child's utterances are shown in *italics*.

Oh, give me something to eat.

No, not yet.

When are you? When are you?

A bit later on when you've had your drink. You've only just had dinner. Haven't you?

Yeah.

What's that? (pointing to a necklace among some jewellery on the table)

Oh, eh, what is it? eh – ring.

No. That's a ring.

Bracelet?

No, that's a bracelet.

Yeah, what's this?

A (pause) a nn, necklace.

Necklace, say what's this.

Necklace.

Child (singing) *Tie me, kangaroo. Mummy, do kangaroos talk?*

I don't know.

How do they talk?

How do you think they talk?

How do they talk?

I've never heard a kangaroo talk I don't think. Have you?

No.

We saw a kangaroo, didn't we?

Yeah, but where was the kangaroo?

In the park, wasn't it?

Yeah.

And what else was there?

What else was there?

Some – monkeys.

Yeah, what else?

And –

And some giraffes.

Giraffes, and what else?

Mother and child continue remembering different types of animals seen at the park and then they discuss the reindeer they saw at the weekend.

What sort of reindeer?

Brown, like Santa Claus's reindeer weren't they?

Yeah. But where's Santa Claus's home?

Oh, it's a long way away.

But where 'bouts? Mum – .

It's in toyland.

What colour toyland?

This led to the mother being asked to list all the colours she could think of and then she turned the conversation to naming the colours of objects in the room. After a while, the child changed the topic to identifying the eye colour of a range of relations.

This type of extended conversation requires lengthy attention to an individual child and the adult has drawn on a wide variety of shared experiences. Neither of these two facilities are available to Nursery staff who are having to cope with a large group of competing children. In addition the child needs to feel at ease and confident throughout the course of the conversation. Hutt *et al.* contend that this type of free-flowing adult/child conversation in Nursery School is a rare event, and evidence from Thomas (1973), Sylva *et al.* (1980) and Tizard *et al.* (1980; 1982; 1983) all points in this direction, so that the widely held view of Nursery staff that they are providing a more enabling verbal climate in the Nursery School, compared with *most* working class children's experiences at home, seems open to doubt.

Chapter 11
Summary and conclusions

In this book we have attempted to describe the experiences of the young children whom we watched in their own homes. The children's activities varied widely with their own tastes, their parents' interests and attitudes. In this final chapter we will summarise briefly the major differences in the children's behaviour and experience attributable to the four independent variables on which our sample selection was based, social class, sex, age and family position. We will then go on to review and discuss more general observations about the young child's life at home and relate this to the parents' attitudes to their children's care and education.

The influence of social class was an aspect of major concern in this study, as so much attention has been paid to it in earlier research, using different techniques and the findings from this research have affected the attitudes of people concerned with the education of the young child. In many ways we found that social class did not operate as strongly as the earlier literature would suggest. The vast majority of the children in our sample were plentifully supplied with toys, working class parents spent as much time talking and interacting with their children as middle class parents. The differences we did find were subtle and qualitative. Middle class parents were more likely to provide their children with toys of educational value, which would develop skills like colour and shape discrimination such as jig-saw puzzles and construction equipment. The middle class children were also more plentifully supplied with books. Middle class children were encouraged to spend more time on activities likely to develop pre-reading, writing and number skills. These differences we considered contributed to the middle class children's superior performance on the Stanford-Binet Intelligence Test. There were also qualitative social class language differences. While expanded explanations, which we have categorised as 'Abstracts' were remarkable by their infrequency across the entire sample, simple 'Instructions' involving naming and labelling were frequently given by both groups of parents. However, we considered that working class parents were sometimes providing 'Instructions' which were redundant to their children, the child had already shown that he knew the particular label his parent was supplying. The novelty of the middle class parents' 'Instructions' appeared to stimulate their children to demand more 'Instructions', to ask more 'What's that?' type questions. While parents from both social classes used what we called 'Options' suggestions or invitations to the child to take part in a new activity, they were more frequently used by middle class parents. 'Options' were an extremely effective way of controlling the child's behaviour. They were often used to stimulate the child into an acceptable activity or to deflect him from a potentially unsocial activity, without recourse to punishment. Middle class parents also offered more praise to their children, working class parents used higher rates of 'Negative' or punishing speech with their children. While what parents accepted as tolerable in their children's behaviour varied widely, generally the children were co-operative, only a third of the children were seen to be smacked in the course of observation, and these children were spread across both social classes.

In our introductory chapter we discussed the findings and conclusions of a number of authors who have examined the responses of parents and children drawn from different social class backgrounds in contrived and experimental settings. We mention that these studies have been criticised; people have argued that the pressures of the settings are themselves contributing to the social class differences which have been found. We would conclude that this criticism is well-founded. In the home, free from these pressures, social class differences in speech and style of interaction are not so marked. We would argue that the preschool setting may have a similar effect, constraining and inhibiting the young working class child, so that, for example, his speech and fantasy play are curtailed, enhancing differences that are not apparent at home. We felt this lack of confidence in the working class parents was also reflected in their attitudes to Play Groups and Nursery Schools. Many more of the middle class attended Play Group, working class children were more likely to attend Nursery School. While the shorter hours of Play Groups combined with the working class mothers relative lack of car transport presented working class parents with more practical problems, working class parents also seemed to be influenced by their feeling that teachers, not parents, were the experts. Therefore, 'teaching' the young child was the responsibility of trained teachers and not of parents.

Sex differences were marked where traditionally sex linked toys were concerned. The boys had more weapons, aeroplanes, trains, cars and petrol pumps; the girls more dolls, cuddly toys and toy domestic paraphernalia. These preferences went beyond their toys, boys incorporated into their activities tools, repair equipment like fuse wire and screws and hardware rubbish items such as old bicycle wheels and pieces of guttering. The boys were more interested in excitement like dustcarts, diggers and aeroplane trails. In contrast, the girls preferred household items which were essentially feminine; jewellery, handbags, make-up, hair rollers and all types of clothing. The boys tended to spend more time in activities involving throwing and climbing, building and construction and vehicle riding; the girls in dressing, climbing and swinging and jumping and placing small objects in and out of containers. The girls also indulged in more fantasy person play or imaginative role play, using domestic roles as their models. Both models and domestic 'props' for this type of play are easily available in the home. Boys, in contrast, tended to favour 'hero' type models, usually television characters they enacted briefly, selecting easily identifiable physical and vocal characteristics, e.g. arms stiffly extended and 'Exterminate, exterminate' for a dalek. Neither mothers nor fathers spent more time playing with either their sons or their daughters. The one activity which fathers engaged in more with their sons than their daughters was football, but they did not spend more time with their sons in rough social physical play and mothers were as likely to engage in this with their children as fathers. The sex of play partners was largely fortuitous for Home children. It depended on the sex of other siblings in the family and whether a girl or boy of the same age happened to be living conveniently nearby. It was impossible in this study to control for the sexes of the siblings; it would have involved an unfeasible inflation of the sample size. Differences may well be more marked in, for example, all male or all female sibships, but we would suggest that the sex difference found in preschool group settings such as boys showing more aggressive and rough physical play, girls more affiliative and caring behaviour, are enhanced when the child is with a large group of mixed sex children and can choose same sexed children as play partners. Maccoby and Jacklin (1975) argue that differential socialisation of boys and girls is a long and continual process. We would agree and conclude that it is not surprising that we found few specific incidents which indicated differential sexual socialisation in a sample period covering a day in the life of the child but, given that children have, for example, already been supplied with sex appropriate toys and clothes, it is not surprising that by the age of three or four years children are already displaying definite sex role identification.

Developmental maturity was clearly marked between the different age bands. Temper tantrums and incidents of weeping, dummy and thumb sucking, and problems over eating all declined with increasing age. The youngest children in the sample were requiring more adult attention, more cuddles and physical attention. However, activity differences according to age are less apparent. Parental expectations of young children's competence varied enormously and were not consistent with social class or the sex of the child. The children's own tastes and interests varied. This prevented clear cut activity differences although the children in the youngest age band were still likely to indulge in more infantile behaviour, like exploring novel objects with concurrent tactile and visual attention, or wriggling and rolling about on the floor. Individual homes do not provide such consistent experience as Nursery Schools, where equipment like sand trays and jig-saw puzzles are readily available and the small children show a clear preference for the sand, the older children for the table toys. Even in such an important area as the child's overall supervision, whether he is allowed to play outside his parent's front gate, the parents' decision is heavily and necessarily influenced by fortuitous neighbourhood pressures; pressures absent from the 'closed' community of the Nursery School.

Family position, to our surprise, had a more potent influence than either social class or sex on social interaction between the subjects and both adults and other children. Youngest children received far less attention from adults and spent far more of their time playing and talking to other children than the other two groups. Only children received most adult attention but Eldest children, despite the fact that they, like Youngest children, had siblings, tended to be closer to Only children in terms of the amount of adult attention they received. Fathers, particularly, ignored their Youngest children, concentrating their attention on older siblings, when they returned from work in the evenings or at weekends. While receiving less adult attention, Youngest children spent far more time than the other two groups playing and talking to other children. Youngest children tended to 'tag' along with older children and to take part in activities which depended on the initiation of an older child, such as games involving them taking turns and following simple rules. This often led to irritation in the older child and Eldest children interacting in turn with their younger siblings showed more physical and verbal aggression than the other two groups. Parents, in turn, told off Eldest children most, partly attributable to these siblings' disputes but also because of their more 'laissez-faire' attitude to Youngest children, who showed a happy-go-lucky attitude to life, laughing more and weeping less than the other two groups. Snow, Jacklin and Maccoby (1981) from a series of experimentally manipulated interactions, comparing 33-month-old Only, Eldest and later born children found that Only children were the most assertive and most social in peer interactions. Later borns were least. In our study, due to their lack of siblings, Only children had far less access to other children, so the Eldest children had far more potential time for aggressive interactions. In line with the findings of Snow *et al.*, is the finding in our study that Only children spent least time watching other people, Youngest children most. In other words, Only children were more likely to become actively involved in another person's activity instead of hanging back watching. Only children also took part less in the childish type of activities, such as play wrestling, tickling and making funny faces. Mothers of Only children stood out in participating more with their children in physical activities such as pushing swings and tricycles, presumably compensating for their child's lack of a sibling participant.

There is a large and inconclusive literature on the effects of family provision. In the largest studies to date of intellectual competence and its relation to family and birth order, Belmont and Marolla (1973) and Zajonc and Markus (1975) showed that intellectual performance declines with increasing family size and that the last born in families of each size shows a greater decline in intellectual performance than any other birth rank. They also found that Only children were not scoring highest but at about the same level as the first born of a four child family. They suggest that both Only and the last born children lack the opportunity to be an 'intellectual resource' or 'teacher' of younger siblings. Our sample is too small to examine the relationship of family size or take into account the age gaps between siblings but the Stanford-Binet results do show (but not significantly) the Youngest children scoring, on average, lower than the other two family positions. Certainly they were receiving less adult attention and Eldest children were having the experience of initiating and controlling social interactions with their younger siblings. Despite the cognitive drawbacks, emotionally, a cheerful Youngest may have his compensation.

Turning from differences between our subsamples, we will now examine more general issues concerning the young child's life at home. We were surprised at how little the majority of children participated in domestic chores with their parents. It is slower and often frustrating to enlist the 'help' of a young child, but as parents were prepared to spend time playing with their children it was not time alone which precluded children from participating in domestic affairs. It is worth examining current sources of parental education. First, television, preschool children's television programmes concentrate on making toys and models, children's games as well as stories and simple documentary films. Children's toys are well advertised on television. If a mother attends Play Group or visits a Nursery School, she is likely to see the children using a variety of types of physical equipment, indulging in messy play, doing puzzles, building with constructional toys, using junk materials for modelling and collage work and looking at a variety of books in the book corner. All these sources of information are highly beneficial in showing parents potentially new activities and experiences which they can give their children, but these are all *child*-centred rather than 'adult' activities. Domestic activities are potentially full of cognitively stimulating experiences for a young child. He can also readily observe that the task is productive by the outcome: that hoovering has cleaned the carpet or shelling peas has contributed to dinner. Young children do derive enormous satisfaction from successfully performing a 'real' task. Taking part in 'adult' chores requires more discipline in the child and provides him with more detailed information about the process involved than in an equivalent pretend game. In a fantasy game a child may happily peel the potatoes after he has cooked the chips, whereas his actions must comply with real demands in domestic activities. While many preschool institutions make great efforts to involve the children in activities such as baking, the fact that it is an organised part of the curriculum divorces the activity from necessity and it is only in the home that the unique opportunities lie for this type of domestic involvement and participation in an aspect of adult life.

Not only does the participation in domestic chores provide the young child at home with opportunities to participate in adult life and the 'real' world but it also provides structured activities which 'guide' and offer ready opportunity to the parent for social interaction with the child. Constructive and fruitful interaction with a young child is not a skill which automatically develops with parenthood. While some adults have an easy ability to engage with a child in an activity, enhancing the activity with their suggestions and participation and using it as a basis for conversation, others cannot or do not feel it appropriate to do this. Where parents were in a situation which provided a ready made structure, conversation increased, for example, with domestic chores and when dressing, bathing and toileting their child. We would suggest that this is an additional reason why fathers choose to play football with their sons, not only is it a traditionally masculine activity, but football is a clearly defined way of playing with a child. Letter and number activities led not only to general talk but also to high rates of 'Instructional' speech. They offer obvious, frequent opportunities for a parent to impart knowledge, to give names, labels and explanations. Only a minority of children had toys and equipment specifically designed for letter and number learning. Instead parents used everyday items, money, road, signs, pencils and paper. When children were looking at books with adults, again the adult was taking part in a 'guided' activity. The pictures and text provide easy prompts. Here again children were likely to receive comparatively high levels of 'Instructional' speech. Dunn, Wooding and Herman (1977) found that when toddlers looked at books and pictures with their mother, at home, the mothers' language was particularly rich in features important to promoting language acquisition.

It is much more difficult for an adult to become actively but sensitively involved in an activity such as fantasy play where the adult must rely entirely on his own imagination and initiative. Despite our finding that parental participation in fantasy play may lead to an increase of this activity, it was not accompanied by high levels of adult/child conversation. Often parental participation was merely acquiesence to a role allotted by the child. In the sister project conducted by Hutt *et al.* (in prep.), in various preschool contexts, they found Nursery staff were similarly reticent in extending or engaging in conversation, when a child had initiated a fantasy activity. While 'messy' play activities, such as foot painting and modelling with plasticine and clay can provide a basis for conversation, relatively few children took part in these types of activities at home. In small terraced or semi-detached houses, space is limited and mothers, very understandably, baulk at the hazards of paint splashes and plasticine working into the living room carpet.

Finally we come to considering parental attitudes to Play Groups and Nursery Schools. A major point is that parents were very ill informed about the preschool facilities available to them in their area. We suspect this lack of information is not confined to parents but exists among some professionals, who come into contact with parents and children and are in a position to advise parents and help spread the information. Certainly we have encountered Head Teachers of Infant Schools, Health Visitors and Social Workers who have not been clear about available facilities, either locally or nationally. We have suggested in Chapter 9 practical ways in which the information could be spread.

As we have pointed out earlier, the working class children were less likely to attend Play Group than the middle class children. Shinman (1981) found that within a relatively homogeneous working class community, mothers who did not use a specifically established Play Group or whose children only attended briefly and sporadically, tended to be women who had married and started their families at a very young age, disliked the neighbourhood, had little or no contact with family or friends and took little pleasure in their children's company. She argues that it is this group which might have benefited most, both the mothers and the children, from Play Group experience. In Stoke-on-Trent, there is a well established tradition, because of the long history of nursery provision, of Nursery School attendance. It was widely accepted, particularly by working class parents, that children did go to Nurseries. Play Groups, like elsewhere, were a relatively recent innovation. Cultural tradition, lack of information and perceived practical problems of taking children for relatively short periods in the day, all seemed to act against working class children attending Play Group. One of the advantages of Play Group is its reliance on parental involvement, but this in itself can deter the less confident mother, particularly, when she feels she will be socially inferior to other mothers there, when for example, a Play Group is drawing children from both a private and a council estate. Arguably, the lack of involvement and responsibility for parents when they send their children to Nursery School can be seen as an advantage by parents with less confidence.

We mentioned in the first chapter that the Consortium on Developmental Continuity (1977) concluded, after a follow up study of selected preschool intervention programmes, that preschool intervention could be shown to have persistent beneficial effect. Experimental children were significantly more likely to meet school requirements than control children, in that they were significantly less likely to be placed in special schools or held back a grade (Consortium for Longitudinal Studies, 1978; Darlington *et al.* 1980). The Consortium considered that possibly a contributory factor to the experimental children's performance was a sustained change in parental attitude. A number of the programmes under examination had incorporated home visiting. Armstrong and Brown (1979), working in this country, followed up a small sample of children five years after the experimental group had received 18 months' home tuition. No measured performance difference was discernible between the experimental and control groups, but the mothers of the experimental children retained more positive attitudes towards learning and education. Douglas (1964) in his longitudinal study of a large nationally selected group of British children, reported that parental interest in the children's school performance, measured by parent/teacher contact, had a marked effect on the children's primary school performance and the children's attainment of grammar school places, (this study was carried out before selective secondary schools had been largely abolished). Douglas considered that the effects of parental interest increased as the child's school career progressed. In a recent study, Tizard, Schofield and Hewison (1982) found that when parents, a few of whom were illiterate and non-English speaking, were encouraged regularly to listen to their children read at home, the children's reading performance improved radically, compared to children who were receiving extra teacher tuition at school. These studies all suggest that involving the parents in the child's nursery or school life is vital to his educational success.

Both Tizard *et al.* (1981) and Cleave *et al.* (1982) describe the difficulties in building up good communication between preschool staff and parents and the misunderstandings and misperceptions that can so easily arise on either side. This often led staff to infer that parents were not interested or concerned with their children. We cannot emphasise strongly enough the love, pride and interest that all the parents in the sample showed towards their children. Nursery staff have a unique opportunity to establish relations with parents at the initial stages of a child's school career, to capitalise on this good-will and boost the parents' own sense of responsibility and confidence in their ability to contribute to their own children's education. As the Plowden Committee (1967) advocated:

> Nursery education should throughout be an affair of co-operation between the Nursery and the home and it will only succeed if it carries the parents into partnership.

Appendices

APPENDIX I

Appendix 1 incorporates:

1. Checklist category definitions
2. Checklist

General conventions
1. Checklist columns refer to time; rows to behaviour categories, environmental surroundings and people, other than the child present.

2. Unless otherwise stated categories were time sampled i.e. a recording indicates that the behaviour etc., was ongoing for the predominant portion of that particular time interval. Several column entries indicate concurrency.

3. Event recording - every individual occurrence of that behaviour is recorded in the appropriate time interval.

4. One zero time sampling - if the behaviour occurs withing a particular time interval it is recorded regardless of frequency or duration.

5. An activity is regarded as one, when it is impossible for its components to be performed independently. When a child is performing more than one of these activities simultaneously then they are separately coded and recorded concurrently.

6. Every time a child uses a new object in a 'play' capacity i.e. excluding categories 'Auto manip +', 'Auto manip -', and 'Functional', it is recorded in the object column and underlined.

7. Personal symbols are attached to an activity regarded as taking place jointly with that individual. The criteria for assessing an activity as 'joint' are:

1   If the activity is durational, the participants' attention to that activity occupies the preponderant length of the time interval.

or

2(a) The individual makes more than one separate statement to the child about the activity during the time interval.

or

2(b) The individual speaks continuously about the activity to the child during the time interval.

8. The 'person' categories are as follows:

Mother	Adult male relative
Father	Adult female non-relative
Adult female relative	Adult male non-relative
Younger female sibling	Elder male sibling
Younger male sibling	Adult female sibling
Elder female sibling	Adult male sibling
Younger female non-sibling	Same age male sibling
Young male non-sibling	Same age female non-sibling
Same age female non-sibling	Same age male non-sibling

Adult = over 16 years; same age = within 9 months of child's own age.

Checklist category definitions

1. Loc/Op (Location and Operational)

B –   public and private buildings, other than included in H, e.g. library, shops, bank, swimming baths, friend's house.

H –   own home, includes garage, outdoor lavatory and outbuildings.

O –   out of doors, i.e. not in any building.

V –   vehicles, e.g. bus, car.

F –   any organised functional or domestic venture from the home
establishment e.g. shopping, taking sibling to school, journey
to and from Play Group, etc.

R –   any organised recreational expedition from the home establishment e.g. shopping, taking sibling to school, journey to
and from Play Group.

A –   adult non-parental caretaker figure (judged by Observer to be
16 years of age or over, approx.) who is in sight and/or same
room as child when $ applies.

S –   in sight and/or same room as parents.

/ –   child out of sight of Observer.

After an initial entry of one of the sub-codes H,O,B, and V, it will
be assumed that the position remains unchanged until one of these
sub-codes appears. F or R are mutually exclusive but may be
recorded concurrently with B,O or V. If F or R follow each other
sequentially, then second code terminates the first, otherwise F or
R act as terminators. S, $ and A operate similarly, being mutually
exclusive and terminating each other./ functions on a normal time
sample basis, with an entry every applicable time interval.

2. *TV (Television etc.)*

Ⓡ–   radio, record player etc., on and transmitting. (R̸ - off)

R –   radio, record player etc., watching or listening to, indicated by
overt behaviour.

Ⓣ–   television on and transmitting. (T̸ - off)

T –   television viewing.

3. *Water/Sand (Water and Sand Play)*

S –   play with sand or soil or any granulated material.

W –   play that requires liquid as an essential element.

4. *Mod/Draw (Soft Modelling and Drawing and Colouring)*

D –   drawing, colouring, scribbling (excluding letters or numbers)

M –   modelling and general manipulation of completely pliant sub-stanced which have no predetermined shape e.g. clay (natural or commercial), flour and water dough, commercial play-dough, plasticine.

5. *Paint/Paste (Painting and String)*

F –   fabric, folding, glueing, cutting or tearing.

P –   painting.

S –   string, find manipulation of string, rope or similar.

6. *Const/Arrange (Construction, Shape and Arrange)*

A –   arranging, matching and shape games, using components to form a self-determined or a predetermined pattern or picture e.g. jigsaws, mosaics.

C –   constructing with interlocking or piling components, e.g. Lego, Playplax, Little Men (Arnold), shoe boxes, or wooden bricks.

P –   packing and unpacking objects into receptacles, where the packing itself appears to be the dominant activity; includes fastening and unfastening of receptacles e.g. transferring marbles from bag to satchel.

7. Fing/Noise (Noise Making and Finger Play)

F – finger play, use of fingers, hands, limbs, body in definite sequence to accord with counting, rhymes, music, songs etc., without body movements.

N – making noises with instrument, hands etc., e.g. blowing.

8. Books (Books and Printed Material)

L – child looking at, examining any printed material.

N – listening to story told by another person, without recourse to book or similar.

R – listening to story read or told from a book or similar by another person; child may be looking at book at the same time.

9. Let/No (Letter/Number and Animals)

A – animal - involved activities, includes speech to animals if it occupies the preponderant portion of the time interval.

L – any activity including speech (if forms preponderant length of time interval) involving letters e.g. spelling outdoor signs, typing, copying adult in writing alphabet, speaking alphabet.

N – any activity, including speech (if it forms preponderant length of time interval) involving numbers e.g. telling time on clock, counting items.

10. Manip (Object Plus and Minus Look)

+ – visually examining, while holding and/or manipulating and exploring, object with hands or feet or mouth.

– – not looking at object while holding, manipulating, mouthing.

F – fiddling, manipulating, while looking at object, but without exploration. (Distinguished from 13U by fine manipulation involved).

11. *Auto Manip (Auto-manipulation and Immobile)*

+ – automanipulate + look, also includes visual inspection of child's own limbs, body, current clothing unaccompanied by manipulation.

– – automanipulate - look, excluding thumb and finger sucking.

I – immobile, child completely motionless, staring into space.

M – mobile, child relatively motionless, gazing unspecifically at surroundings.

T – thumbsucking, including any finger sucking.

12. *Sort (Sort, Prepare and Clear Toys and Play Activities)*

C – clear, putting object away.

P – prepare, may involve collecting, carrying, adjusting, objects essential to a future or ongoing activity. If the child's behaviour has not indicated that an object is 'essential to a future or ongoing activity', then Travel and Manipulate - Look, for example, may be recorded.

S – sort (physical) e.g. sorting through items in box/pile/ cupboard. Includes searching round room/house for items.

13. *Ball (Ball Games)*

B – Kicking and/or throwing and/or heading etc., includes locomotor time (may include use of instrument).

M – miniature physical activities which are performed by the child abiding by local or conventional social rules or constraints.

U – unrestrained miniature physical activities e.g. child waving weed round head, knocking two toys together.

14. Phys Obj (Physical Play Object Oriented)

F – climbing, swinging, bouncing on furniture and outdoor objects e.g. jumping off armchair, walking on top of wall, using climbing frame or slide.

I – inside, or under, sufficiently large object, while concurrently performing another activity e.g. sitting in paper bag watching TV, playing with doll in cupboard; sitting on stationary swing, watching traffic.

O – occupant, child in or on V type objects and being pushed by another individual, or not itself involved in the propulsion.

P – push-pull, free-swinging or vehicular objects e.g. pram, trolley, cardboard box plus string, swing, seesaw.

V – vehicle driving and gross physical repetitive play movements, e.g. tricycle, scooter, moonhopper, pedalcar, glide-about vehicles, objects large enough for the child to be in or on and propel, swings, rocking horses and umbrellas.

15. Phys Loc (Physical Whole Body - Locomotor)

B – whole body movements e.g. rolling on ground, turning somersaults.

L – locomotor activities, any locomotor activity which the child chooses to perform independently or in excess to that demanded by another individual e.g. child rambling about on allotment; child skipping beside mother on way to Play Group.

T –   any locomotor activity performed according to the constraints of another individual e.g. walking to shops with mother, running beside mother to catch bus.

V –   vehicle, occupation of unpowered vehicle for functional travel e.g. going shopping in pram or pushchair, may be stationary or mobile.

16. Dress Up (Dressing Up)

Child dressing up in clothes and articles not normally worn by itself or inappropriate to that particular occasion; either a specific commercial kit or jumble and application of conventional make-up, e.g. father's old jersey or a 'nurse's uniform' or sunglasses worn in the house.

D –   dressing up, when the items are being actively used in the course of play.

/ –   indicates a dressing up article is being worn.

⧸ –   indicates dressing up article has ceased to be worn.

17. Rep Obj (Representational Object Fantasy Play)

Use of representational objects e.g. toy models of adult objects and real adult objects in conventional simulated situations, e.g. push MT along making motor noises; siting in parent's car, twisting steering wheel and making car noises.

18. Fant Obj (Fantasy Object Play)

Object changes character in child's imagination and is used in its imaginative capacity, e.g. table becomes house, ball becomes doll, Lego becomes gun, jigsaw pieces become car. State object used and its imaginative identity in object column.

19. Fant Person (Fantasy Person Play)

Child or other people participating change character in the child's imagination, e.g. child becomes a cowboy. State child's or other other individual's identity in object column.

20. Immat Fant (Immaterial Fantasy Play)

Play includes fantasy people or objects which have no substantive identity in the environment, e.g. child talks to non-existent people such as a co-pilot, feeds non-existent horse.

21. Ingest (Ingestion)

I –   main meals, breakfast, lunch, tea, supper, dinner.

S –   snacks, e.g. sweets, biscuits or fruit not eaten in connection with a main meal.

22. Dining/Games

– indicates dining has begun (–, it has finished). Dining includes actual eating, sitting in a formal manner and sitting in a formal manner before or after eating and between courses. If the child or another participant leaves the table while eating or stops eating and performs an unrelated activity at the table their participation in 'Dining' ceases.

G – indicates game-playing has begun (ϕ, it has finished). A game is being played if the participatns are operating under explicit rules, which must be obeyed for the game to continue e.g. Grandmother's footsteps, Snap.

23. Domestic (Domestic Activity)

C –   cooking, preparation of food for general consumption; includes time child spends collecting and preparing necessary implements for this e.g. peeling vegetables, mixing ingredients.

F – fetching, moving, opening (including attempts) items and performing chores and errands for other people e.g. putting away cake tins, delivering messages, moving chair to reach sink or cupboard.

M – maintenance, general household and garden maintenance, includes washing and drying clothes and dishes, polishing, dusting, bed-making, cleaning windows.

P – preparation of food for own immediate consumption e.g. unwrapping own sweets, cutting up own food at meal times, getting own drink.

24. Func (Functional Toilet Activity)

A – assistance; child is assisting another person, functionally, e.g. wiping somebody else's nose.

B – bathing, active washing, with or without assistance, involving main part of body under water.

D – dress/undress, includes any article of apparel.

H – hygiene and medicine, includes washing or drying self, warming self, hair-brushing, teeth cleaning, nail cutting, wiping nose, eyes, hands.

L – lavatory, if the child is on the lavatory, potty or similar.
If the child is briefly out of sight and the Observer deduces the lavatory is being used, then L is recorded; however, if there is any doubt the child is recorded as being out of sight. If the child is in view and performs another activity while on the lavatory etc., this is recorded concurrently.

S – sleeping or resting, relative immobility with eyes closed.

25. *Social (Social Play)*

G – gross social physical play, involving body/limbs contact with another individual e.g. adult throwing child in air.

H – hide self or object from particular person, in which case the respective person code is used.

M – miniature social physical play - activities which depend on the social communication in another person's movements and facial expressions. This may incorporate the subsidiary use of an object to enhance or facilitate the effect of the above, e.g. spoons in mouth plus laughter and movement; fitting hoop-la rings on arms and/or head; peeking round door; tickling; making faces at each other; blowing at each other.

26. *Watch (Watching)*

P – observing person/people engaging in an activity in which the child is not a constant participant.

I – visually examining an inanimate object, which may be moving or stationary e.g. water gushing down storm drain, objects displayed in shop windows.

S – self, watching own reflection.

W – looking through window.

27. *Laugh/Weep (Laughing and Weeping)*

L – laughing.

W – weeping.

Time sampling - one zero.

28. *Oral (Vocal/Oral)*

A –   auto-talk - talking to oneself.

C –   communication, any form of speech except moaning or aggressive speech to another individual.

G –   aggressive spech or vocalisations to another individual.

M –   moaning, persistent whining, vocal and verbalisation.

P –   positive, approval, praise, affection, promise of treats.

S –   singing, humming, reciting, and whistling.

T –   telephone.

Time sampling - one zero.

29. *Speech Adult*

/ –   any form of speech to the Subject except that covered by N
and P specifically.

N –   negative speech to the Subject, includes direct verbal punishment and aggression and threats.

P –   positive speech, approval, praise, affection, promise of treats.

Time sampling - one zero.

30. *Speech Child (not the Subject)*

/ –   any form of speech to the Subject except that covered by N
and P specifically.

N –   negative speech to the Subject, includes direct verbal punishment and aggression and threats.

P – positive speech, approval, praise, affection and promise of treats.

Time sampling - one zero

31. *Commun Others (Communication of Other Individuals to Subject*

A – abstract explanations, a statement or question which involves an abstraction to a class of individuals, objects or events, i.e.. which includes a general principle.

I – giving of information, which may be used outside the child's own home (i.e. excluding specific localised events) which does not involve elaboration or expansion of a concept; such as specifically naming objects by drawing the child's attention to them, making statements of fact without justification, correcting the child's speech to the individual's own speech criteria.

O – option, an invitation, a suggestion to the Subject that he does something - includes non-verbal communication.

R – rejection, rejection of option initiated by the Subject - includes non-verbal communication.

Time sampling - one zero.

32. *Commun (Communication by Subject to Other Individuals)*

A – abstract request.

D – demand for an 'Option'.

I – request for an 'Instruction'.

O – 'Option' from Subject to another individual.

R –   rejection by Subject of another individual's 'Option' - includes non-verbal communication.

Time sampling - one zero

33. *Phys Cont (Physical Contact)*

F –   functional, specific functional physical contact with the child, for example when holding hands or being carried across the street, but excluding physical contact incidental to another activity e.g. in the course of washing the child's face.

P –   positive affective physical contact, such as hugging, hand-holding, cuddling, sitting on a lap.

W –   wrestling, negative durational physical contact.

34. *Neg/Temper (Negative/Temper)*

N –   negative (aggressive or punishing), constraining another individual in a particular place or situation.

-N –   negative (aggressively or punishingly), being constrained in a particular place or situation e.g. being sent to bedroom, shut in cupboard.

S –   show, display object to person.

T –   temper tantrum, muscular rigidity, holding breath, repeated violent movements, hurling body on to floor, head banging, shouting and screaming, hurling objects.

35. *Event (Event Recording)*

A –   accidental injury to Subject.

D –   destroy, take, knock object from another individual.

K – kiss.

N – negatively affective brief physical or symbolic injury e.g. blow with hand or foot, bit hit with implement, symbolic injury, spitting, rude face.

T – temper flash, a brief incident of 34 T.

-D – have object destroyed, taken or knocked by another individual.

-N – negative affective brief physical or symbolic injury by another individual e.g. as in N.

Checklist

| NO | SESS | DATE |
| | | |

TIME	0		1		2		3		4	
Loc/Op B H O V F F R R A S S /										
TV ℝ R R ① T T										
Water/Sand S W										
Mod/Draw D M										
Paint/Paste F P S										
Const/Arrange A C P										
Fing/Noise F N										
Books L N R										
Let/No A L N										
Manip + – F										
Auto Manip + – I M T										
Sort C P S										
Ball B M U										
Phys Obj F I O P V										
Phys Loc B L T V										
Dress Up D / +										
Rep Obj										
Fant Obj										
Fant Person										
Immat Fant										
Ingest I S										
Dining / + G Ꞡ										
Domestic C F M P										
Func A B D H L S										
Social G H M										
Watch I P S W										
Laugh/Weep L W										
Oral A C G M P S T										
Speech Adult / N P										
Speech Child / N P										
Commun Others A I O R										
Commun Subj. A D I O R										
Phys Cont F P W										
Neg/Temper N – N S T										
Event A D K N T – D – K – N										

APPENDIX II
Selected items from interview and assessment coding manual

26. Occupancy rate was calculated by the number of people divided by the number of rooms. Rooms were assessed in terms of the census 1970 definitions.

36. Dummy use

> *N –* no evidence of dummy use at all
>
> *S –* evidence that child used someone else's dummy regularly as a comfort object.
>
> *Y –* evidence child owns a dummy.

Night nappy

> *Y –* evidence for nappy worn at night.
>
> *N –* no evidence for above

Eating problems

> *Y –* parent has expressed concern about child's food intake.
> *N –* no concern expressed.

Sleeping arrangements

G – goes to bed happily on own or with sibling.

NG – will not go to bed as above e.g. has to fall asleep downstairs; parent has to stay with child till asleep; will not go till parents' own bedtime.

Comfort object

Y – uses object assessed as functioning as 'classical comfort object' i.e. repeated use of specific objects, particularly when stressed or tired.

N – no use of any object in above manner.

40. *Family cleanliness scale*

1. Dirty house smell
2. Floor covering soiled, covered in bits, crumbs.
3. Floor covering as (2), in *more* than one room.
4. Kitchen sink, draining board, work surfaces, cupboard doors have not been washed for considerable period of time.
5. Stove, fridge or other kitchen appliances have not been cleaned for a considerable period of time.
6. Saucepans, cooking implements, cutlery or crockery showing ingrained dirt and food remnants from previous meals.
7. Lavatory, bath or basin show ingrained dirt.
8. Bed linen, furnishings or furniture soiled.
9. Garden or yard uncared for and strewn with rubbish.
10. Parent's or children's clothing show ingrained dirt.
11. Children's hair matted and unbrushed and/or child appears not to have been washed overnight on more than one occasion; parents assessed similarly.

APPENDIX III
Preliminary programming treatment of the checklist data

Paul Collis

The data were primarily composed of the subjects' behaviour recorded in six separate time periods (sessions); each session was of one hour's duration and was further sub-divided into 120 half-minute intervals. The interval is the base time unit of the study and activities recorded during the period give rise to a single observation. Initially 150 categories were thought adequate to define the child's behaviour and a number of environmental factors to be measured in the study. In conventional statistical terms the number of characters required, at the minimum, to define this data for 200 children is 22 million, which if coded on to cards would require 400,000 records, which is unmanageable.

The major contribution to the size of the data, within an observation, is the recording of (on average) 130 variables (activities) to be absent. The project becomes more manageable if, rather than record the absence or presence of an activity, only those activities which are present are recorded - the non-presence of an activity implies its absence. Conventionally the value of a variable is indicated by position within the observation (record); to record only those activities which are present requires some means of 'identifying' the activity. The use of identifiers to be associated with an activity was estimated to produce a saving of 80 per cent on the size of the original data.

After coding the data in this form a new step is involved in the analysis. The coded data needs to be pre-processed to convert it into a form suitable for conventional statistical programs. This approach produces the 22 M byte file described. Much of the statistical survey would not require individual period observations, but more manageable 'derived data', such as accumulated frequencies for a session. Thus the program to pre-process the coded data needs to provide two forms of the data: the expanded file (22 M bytes; 288,000 observations) and the derived frequencies file (0.6 M bytes; 1,200 observations).

A series of enhancements was designed to further ease the problems of coding and reduce the size of the base data. Some identifiers were termed as 'ongoing' e.g. 'radio on', which once defined, act for subsequent periods until explicitly switched off. This concept was used to code biographic child data such as age and sex and session data such as time and date of observation.

The particular example of the radio also exemplifies a further class of identifier, which is really a superset of the class 'ongoing', called 'mutually exclusive'. The presence of the 'radio off' identifier automatically 'switches off' the 'radio on' identifier, thus the two identifiers 'radio off' and 'radio on' are mutually exclusive. The types of identifiers which can thus be defined to (and interpreted by) the preprocessor are 'simple', 'ongoing' and 'mutually exclusive'.

Most of the identifiers, as mentioned above, are dichotomous, and in the expansion of the coded data into the expanded file the preprocessor inserts a value of one (1) if the identifier is present and zero ($\emptyset$) if it is absent. The value which is inserted into the expanded file can be explicitly stated by enclosing the value in brackets after the identifier. This construct was particularly necessary for identifiers such as 'time of day', 'child number' and 'date', and event recorded behavioural data.

A further requirement was identified, involving the association of 'simple' identifiers (e.g. 'sand play', with 'mother'). This problem could not be solved by permutating all the possible associated activities to form new identifiers and so they were associated by 'bracketing' variables. A final requirement, which does not alter the logic of the preprocessor, was to repeat consecutive periods.

The preprocessing program needs to check that all input data is meaningful and have the option to verify newly coded data without the function of the expanded and the frequencies files. This gave rise to two modes of working. To assist verification of the data a hierarchy of constructs was defined to prevent the propagation of errors determined by the program.

An example of two hypothetical intervals follows to show the form of the data:

ARE: Being read to (Group A, 'being READ to')

BTH: Thumb or finger sucking (Group B, 'THUMB')
LP: Affectionate physical contact (Group L, 'PHYSICAL')
M: Mother (person code, MOTHER)
/:   Interval terminator

Example   BTH, (ARE, LP, M) / *2
            The child is sucking his thumb, while being read to by
            his mother, sitting on her lap. The behaviour continues
            for two intervals.

In practice the identifiers were chosen to be a maximum of three
characters in length but the program will deal with identifiers up to
ten characters long.

References

ALTMANN, J. (1974) 'Observational study of behaviour: sampling methods', *Behaviour,* 49 (3/4), 227-67.

ARMSTRONG, G. and BROWN, F. (1979). *Five Years On.* Oxford: Social Evaluation Unit.

BECHTEL, R. B., ACHELPOL, C. and ACKERS, R. (1972). 'Children's use of television and other media'. *Television and Social Behaviour Vol. IV. Reports and Papers. TV in Day-to-Day Life: Patterns of Use.* 274-301

BELMONT, L. and MAROLLA, F.A. (1973). 'Birth order, family size and intelligence'. *Science,* 182, 1096.

BEREITER, C. and ENGELMANN, S. (1966). *Teaching disadvantaged children in preschool.* Engelwood Cliffs, New Jersey: Prentice-Hall.

BERNSTEIN, B. (1971). 'Social class and linguistic development: a theory of social learning'. In: HALSEY, A.H., FLOUD, J. and ANDERSON, C.A. (Eds). *Education, Economy and Society.* Glencoe, Illinois: Free Press.

BERNSTEIN, B. (1971). *Class, Codes and Control. Vol I.* London: Routledge & Kegan Paul.

BERNSTEIN, B. (1972). *Class, Codes and Control. Vol II.* London: Routledge & Kegan Paul.

BERNSTEIN, B. (1975). *Class, Codes and Control. Vol III.* London: Routledge & Kegan Paul.

BIBLOW, E. (1973). 'Imaginative play and the control of aggressive behaviour'. In: SINGER, J.L. *The Child's World of Make-Believe.* New York: Academic Press.

BLANK, M. AND SOLOMON, F. (1969). 'How shall the disadvantaged child be taught?' *Child Development,* 40,47-61.

BLOOM, B. (1964). *Stability and Change in Human Characteristics.* London: John Wiley & Sons, Inc.

BRYANT, B., HARRIS, M. and NEWTON, D. (1980). *Children and Minders.* Oxford Preschool Research Project. London: Grant McIntyre.

CAREW, J.V., CHAN, I. and HALFAR, C. (1976). *Observing Intelligence in Young Children: eight case studies.* Englewood Cliffs, New Jersey: Prentice-Hall.

CAREW, J.V. (1980). 'Experience and the development of intelligence in young children at home and in day care'. *Mongraphs of the Society for Research in Child Development,* 45 (6-7, Serial No. 187).

CICIRELLI, V.G., GRANGER, R.L. *et al.,* (1969). *The Impact of Headstart: an Evaluation of the Effects of Headstart on Children's Cognitive and Affective Development, Vol 1.* Washington, D.C.: Westinghouse Learning Corporation and Ohio University.

CITY OF STOKE-ON-TRENT (1960). *The Jubilee Edition of the Official Handbook.* Cheltenham and London: J. Burrow & Co. Ltd.

CITY OF STOKE-ON-TRENT (1977). *Official Handbook.*

CLARKE-STEWART, K.A. (1973). 'Interactions between mothers and young children: characteristics and consequences'. *Monographs of the Society for Research in Child Development,* 38, (6-7, Serial No. 153).

CLARKE-STEWART, K.A. (1980). Commentary and Reply. In: Carew, J.V. 'Experience and the development of intelligence in young children at home and in day care'. *Monographs of the Society for Research in Child Development,* 45, (6-7, Serial No. 187).

CLEAVE, S., JOWETT, S. and BATE, M. (1982). *And so to school.* Windsor, Berks.: NFER-NELSON.

CONSORTIUM ON DEVELOPMENTAL CONTINUITY (1977). Education Commission of the States: *The Persistence of Preschool Experiments. A long-term Follow-up of Fourteen Infant and Preschool Experiments.* Washington, DC.: DHEW Publication No. (OHDS) 78-30130.

CONSORTIUM FOR LONGITUDINAL STUDIES (1978). Education Commission of the States: *Lasting Effects after Preschool.* Washington, DC.: DHEW Publication No. (OHDS) 79-30178.

DARLINGTON, R.B., ROYCE, J.M., SNIPPER, A.S., MURRAY, H.W. and LAZAAR, I. (1980). 'Preschool programs and later school competence of children from low income families'. *Science.* 208, 202-204.

DAVIE, R., BUTLER, N. and GOLDSTEIN, H. (1972). *From Birth to Seven. A Report of the National Child Development Study.* London: Longman.

DEPARTMENT OF EDUCATION AND SCIENCE (DES) (1972). *White Paper, Education: A Framework for Expansion.* Cmmd. 5174. London: HMSO.

DEWEY, J. (1900). *Elementary School Record.* University of Chicago.

DI PIETRO, J.A. (1981). 'Rough and Tumble Play: A function of gender'. *Developmental Psychology,* 17, No.1, 50-58.

DOUGLAS, J. (1964). *The Home and the School.* London: Mac-Gibbon & Kee.

DOWLING, M. (1976). *The Modern Nursery.* London: Longman.

DUNN, J. and KENDRICK, C. (1980). 'The arrival of a Sibling. Changes in patterns of interactions between mother and first born child.' *Journal of Child Psychology andd Psychiatry,* 21, 119-132.

DUNN, J. and KENDRICK, C. (1981). 'Interaction between young siblings: Association with the interaction between mother and first born child'. *Developmental Psychology,* 17, 3, 336-343

DUNN, J., WOODING, C. and HERMAN, J. (1977). 'Mothers' speech to young children: variation in context.' *Developmental Medical Child Neurology,* 19, 629-638.

DUNN, L.M., HORTON, K.B. and SMITH, J.O. (1968). Peabody Language Development Kits. Minnesota: American Guidance Services, Inc.

EAST NEWCASTLE ACTION GROUP SURVEY (1971). *Working-class Mothers and Preschool Education: Attitudes to Nursery Schools in a Working-class Community.*

EIFFERMANN, R.R. (1971). Social play in childhood. In: HERRON, R.E. SUTTON-SMITH, B. (Eʃs). *Child's Play.* New York: Wiley.

EMMERICH, W. (1971). *Structure and development of personal - social behaviours in preschool settings.* Educational Testing Service – Head Start Longitudinal Study.

FAIRWEATHER, H. (1976). 'Sex differences in cognition'. *Cognition,* 4, 231-280.

FEITELSON, D. (1972). 'Developing imaginative play in preschool as a possible approach to fostering creativity'. *Early Child*

Development and Care, 1, 181-195

FEITELSON, D. and ROSS, G.S. (1973). 'The neglected factor – play'. *Human Development,* 16, 202-224.

FERGUSON, G.A. (1971). *Statistical Analysis in Psychology and Education. 3rd Edition.* Tokyo: McGraw-Hill Book Co, 185.

FLETCHER, S.S. and WALTON, S. (Translators), (1912). *Froebel's Chief Writings on Education.* London: Edward Arnold, 178.

FREYBERG, J.T. (1973). 'Increasing the imaginative play of urban disadvantaged kindergarten children through systematic training.' In: SINGER, J.L. *The Child's World of Make-believe,* New York: Academic Press.

FROEBEL, See under FLETCHER and WALTON.

GOLOMB, C. and CORNELIUS, C.B. (1977). 'Symbolic play and its cognitive significance'. *Developmental Psychology,* 13, 3, 246-252.

GREAT BRITAIN. DEPARTMENT OF EDUCATION & SCIENCE. (1972). *Education: A framework for expansion.* London: HMSO.

GRIFFING, P. (1980). 'The relationship between socioeconomic status and sociodramatic play among black kindergarten children'. *Genetic Psychology Monographs,* 101, 3-34.

GUILFORD, J.P. (1965). *Fundamental Statistics in Psychology and Education, 4th Edition.* New York: McGraw-Hill.

HALVERSON, C.F. & WALDROP, M.F. (1973). 'The relations of mechanically recorded activity level to varieties of preschool play behaviour'. *Child Development,* 44, 678-681.

HARTUP, W.W. (1974) 'Aggression in childhood: Developmental perspectives'. *American Psychologist,* 29, 336-341.

HESS, R.D. and SHIPMAN, V.C. (1965). 'Early experience and the socialisation of cognitive modes in children'. *Child Development,* 36, 869-886.

HUGHES, M., MAYALL, B., MOSS, P., PERRY, J., PETRIE, P. and PINKERTON, G. (1980) *Nurseries Now.* Harmondsworth: Penguin.

HUNT, J. McV. (1961). *Intelligence and Experience.* New York: Ronald Press.

HUTT, C. (1979). 'Play in the under-fives: form, development and funtion.' In: HOWELLS, J.G. (Ed) *Modern Perspectives in the Psychiatry of Infancy.* New York: Brunner/Mazel.

HUTT, S.J., HUTT, C., TYLER, S.T. and FOY, H,. (in preparation) *A Natural History of the Preschool.*

ISAACS, S. (1930). *Intellectual Growth in Young Children. The Behaviour of Young Children, Vol 1.* London: Routledge.

ISAACS, S. (1933) *Social Development in Young Children, a Study of Beginnings.* London: Routledge.

KAGAN, J. (1966). 'Reflection-impulsivity: the generality and dynamics of conceptual tempo'. *Journal of Abnormal Psychology,* 71, 17-24.

KLACKENBERG, G. (1949). 'Thumbsucking, Frequency and Etiology'. *Pediatrics,* 4, 418.

KLINGER, E. (1971). *Structure and Functions of Fantasy.* New York: Wiley.

LABOV, W. (1969). 'The logic of nonstandard English.' In: KEDDIE, N. (Ed.) (1973) *Tinker Tailor.* London: Penguin Education.

LANGLOIS, J.H., GOTTFRIED, N.W. and SEAY, B. (1973). 'The influence of sex of peer on the social behaviour of preschool children.' *Developmental Psychology,* 8, 93-98.

LEACH, P. (1975). *Babyhood.* Harmondsworth: Penguin Books.

LEWIS, M. (1969). 'Infants' responses to facial stimuli during the first year of life.' *Psychology,* I, 75-86.

LEWIS, M. (1972). 'State as an infant-environment interaction: analysis of mother-infant behaviour as a function of sex.' *Merrill-Palmer Quarterly,* 18, 95-121.

LYLE, J. and HOFFMAN, H.R. (1972). Children's use of television and other media. *Television and Social Behaviour, Vol. IV. Reports and Papers. TV in Day-to-Day Life: Patterns of Use.* 129-256.

LYTTON, H. and ZWIRNER, W. (1975) 'Compliance and its controlling stimuli observed in a natural setting.' *Developmental Psychology,* 11, 769-779.

LYTTON, H. (1979). 'Disciplinary encounters between young boys and their mothers and their fathers. Is there a contingency system?' *Developmental Psychology,* 15, 256-268.

MacCAULEY, R.K.S. (1977). 'The Myth of female superiority in languages.' *Journal of Child Language,* 5, 353-363

MacDONALD, H.M. (In preparation). *Sex Differences in Verbal Ability. A Review.*

McCARTHY, D. (1954). Language Development in children. In:

Carmichael, L. (Ed.) *Manual of Child Psychology, 2nd Edn.* New York: Wiley.

McCREESH, J. and MAHER, A. (1976) *Preschool Education; Objectives and Techniques.* London: Ward Lock Educational.

McMILLAN, M. (1904). *Education Through the Imagination.* London: Swan Sommeschein.

MACCOBY, E.E. and JACKLIN, C.N. (1975). *The Psychology of Sex Differences.* California: Stanford University Press; London: OUP.

MARSHALL, H.R. and DOSHI, R. (1965). 'Aspects of experience revealed through the doll play of preschool children.' *Journal of Psychology,* 6, 47-57.

MARSHALL, H.R. and HAHN, S.C. (1967). 'Experimental modifications of dramatic play.' *Journal Pers Soc Psychology,* 5, 119-122.

MONTESSORI, M. (1936). *The Secret of Childhood.* London: Longman.

MOSS, P., TIZARD, J. and CROOK, J. (1973). 'Families and their needs.' *New Society.* 23, 638-640.

NEWSON, J. and NEWSON, E. (1963). *Infant Care in an Urban Community.* London: Allen and Unwin.

NEWSON, J. and NEWSON, E. (1968). *Four Years Old in an Urban Community* London: Allen & Unwin.

NEWSON, J. and NEWSON, E. (1976). *Seven Years Old in the Home Environment.* London: Allen & Unwin.

PIAGET, J. (1951). *Play, Drama and Imitation in Childhood.* New York: Norton.

PLOWDEN REPORT. Great Britain. Department of Education and Science. Central Advisory Council for Education (England). (1967).*Children and their primary schools.* London: HMSO

POLLAK, M. (1972). *Today's Three-year-olds in London.* London: Heinemann Medical Books/Spastics International Medical Publications.

POULTON, G.A. and JAMES, T. (1975). *Preschool Learning in the Community. Strategies for Change.* London: Routledge & Kegan Paul.

PRINGLE, M.L.K., BUTLER, N.R. and DAVIE, R. (1966). *11,000 Seven-Year Olds.* London: Longman.

REGISTRAR GENERAL (1970) *Classification of Occupations.* London: Office of Population Censuses and Surveys. HMSO.

ROSEN, C.E. (1974). 'The effects of sociodramatic play on problem-solving behaviour among culturally disadvantaged preschool children.' *Child Development,* 45, 4, 920-927.

ROSEN, H. (1973). *Language and Class: A critical look at the theories of Basil Bernstein.* Bristol: Falling Wall Press.

SALTZ, E. and JOHNSON, J. (1974). 'Training for thematic-fantasy play in culturally disadvantaged children: preliminary results.' *Journal Educational Psychology,* 66, 623-630.

SALTZ, E., DIXON, D. and JOHNSON, J. (1977). 'Training disadvantaged preschoolers on various fantasy activities: effects on cognitive functioning and impulse control.' *Child Development,* 48, 920-927.

SCHEFFÉ, H.A. (1953). 'A method for judging all possible contrasts in the analysis of variance.' *Biometrika,* 40, 87-104.

SCHMUKLER, D. and NAVEH, I. (1980). 'Modification of imaginative play in preschool children through the intervention of an adult model.' *S African Journal of Psychology,* 10, (3/4)

SEARS, R.R. RAUL, L. and ALPERT, R. (1965) *Identification and Child Rearing.* Stanford, California: Stanford University Press.

SHERROD, L. and SINGER, J.L. (1977). 'The development of make-believe play.' In GOLDSTEIN J. (Ed.) *Sports, Games and Play.* New Jersey: Erebaum, 1-28.

SHINMAN, S. (1981). *A chance for every child.* London/New York: Tavistock Publications.

SINGER, J.L. (1961) 'Imagination and waiting ability in childhood.' *Journal of Personality,* 29, 396-413.

SINGER, J.L. (1973). *The Child's World of Make-believe.* New York: Academic Press.

SINGER, J.L. and SINGER, D. (1973). 'Some characteristics of make-believe play in nursery school children: an observational study.' In: SINGER, J.L. (Ed). *The Child's World of Make-believe.* New York: Academic Press.

SINGER, J.L. and SINGER, D.G. (1976). 'Imaginative play and pretending in early childhood: some experimental approaches.' In: DAVIDS, A. (Ed) (1976) *Psychopathology: Current Topics.* Vol 3. New York, London, Sydney, Toronto: John Wiley & Sons, 69-112.

SMILANSKY, S. (1968). *The Effects of Sociodramatic play on Disadvantaged Preschool Children.* New York: John Wiley.

SMITH, P.K. and DODSWORTH, C. (1978). 'Social class differences in the fantasy play of preschool children.' *Journal of Genetic Psychology*, 133, 183-190.

SMITH, P.K. and SYDALL, S. (1978) 'Play and non-play tutoring in preschool children: is it play or tutoring which matters?' *British Journal of Educational Psychology*, 48, 3, 315-325.

SNOW, M., JACKLIN, C., MACCOBY, E. (1981) 'Birth order differences in peer sociability at 33 months.' *Child Development*, 52, 589-595.

SPOCK, B. (1955). *Baby and Child Care*. London: Bodley Head.

SUTTON-SMITH, B. and ROSENBERG. B.G. (1970). *The Sibling*. New York: Holt, Reinhart and Winston.

SYLVA, K. ROY, C. & PAINTER, M. (1980). *Childwatching at Playgroup and Nursery School*. London: Grant McIntyre.

TERMAN, L. and TYLER, L. (1954). 'Psychological Sex Differences.' In: Carmichael, L. (Ed.) *Manual of Child Psychology*. *2nd Edn*. New York: John Wiley.

THOMAS, V. (1973). 'Children's use of language in the Nursery.' *Education Research* 15, 3, 209-216.

TIZARD, B. (1974). 'Do social relationships affect language development?' In: Connolly, K. and Bruner, J. (Eds.) *The Growing Competence*. London/New York: Academic Press.

TIZARD, B., CARMICHAEL, H., HUGHES, M., and PINKERTON, G. (1980). 'Four year olds talking to mothers and teachers.' In: Hersov, L.A. and Berger, M. (Eds.) *Language and Language Disorders in Childhood*. A book supplement to the *Journal of Child Psychology and Psychiatry*, 2, 49-76. Oxford: Pergamon.

TIZARD, B., CARMICHAEL, H., HUGHES, M. and PINKERTON, G. (1982) 'Adult's cognitive demands at home and at nursery school.' *Journal of Child Psychology and Psychiatry*, 23, 105-116.

TIZARD, B., HUGHES, M., CARMICHAEL, H. and PINKERTON, G. (1983). 'Children's questions and adults' answers.' *Journal of Child Psychology and Psychiatry*, 24, 269-281.

TIZARD, B., MORTIMORE, J. and BURCHELL, B. (1981). *Involving Parents in Nursery and Infant Schools*. London: Grant McIntyre.

TIZARD, B., PHILPS, J. and PLEWIS, I. (1976). 'Play in preschool centres I. Play measures and their relation to age, sex and

IQ.' *Journal of Child Psychology and Psychiatry,* 17, 251-264.

TIZARD, B., PHILPS, J. and PLEWIS, I. (1976) 'Play in pre-school centres II. Effects on play of the child's social class and of the educational orientation of the centre.' *Journal of Child Psychology and Psychiatry,* 17, 265-274.

TIZARD, J., SCHOFIELD, W., and HEWISON, J. (1982) 'Collaboration between teachers and parents in assisting children's reading.' *British Journal of Educational Psychology,* 52, 1-15.

TRAISMAN, A.A. and TRAISMAN, H.S. (1958). 'Thumb and finger-sucking: a study of 2,650 infants and children.' *Journal of Paediatrics,* 52, 566-579.

TOUGH, J. (1973). *The Language of Young Children in Education in the Early Years.* University College of Swansea.

TOUGH, J. (1977). *The Development of Meaning.* London: Unwin Educational Books.

VAN DER EYKEN, W. (1977). *The Preschool Years.* 4th Edn. Harmondsworth: Penguin.

WELLS, G. (1978). 'Language use and educational success: an empirical response to Joan Tough's "The Development of Meaning" (1977).' *Research in Education,* 18, 9-34.

WHITING, B. and EDWARDS, C. (1973) 'A cross-cultural analysis of sex differences in the behaviour of children aged 3 through 11'. *Journal of Social Psychology,* 91, 177-188.

WINER, B.J. (1970). *Statistical Principles in Experimental Design.* 2nd Edn. New York: McGraw-Hill.

WOOD, D., McMAHON, L. and CRANSTOUN, Y. (1980). *Working with Under Fives.* London: Grant McIntyre.

WOOTTON, A.J. (1974). 'Talk in the homes of young children.' *Sociology,* 8, 277-295.

YARDLEY, A. (1973). *Young Children Thinking.* London: Evans.

ZAJONC, R.B. and MARCUS, G.B. (1975). 'Birth order and intellectual development.' *Psychological Review,* 82, 1, 74-78.

Index